Singing Bowl Handbook

Eva Rudy Jansen & Dick de Ruiter

Singing Bowl Handbook

Singing Bowls • Tingshaws • Bell • Dorje

Binkey Kok Publications – Haarlem/The Netherlands

Translation: Tony Langam, Dick de Ruiter et al.
Editing: Valerie Cooper
Cover design and interior design: Jaap Koning, Amsterdam
Photographs: G. Boer, Eelco Boeijinga, Benelux Press, Mathieu Mentink, Danny Becher (pages 42, 43, 44 and 45)
Singing bowls shown in this book: collection of Binkey Kok (Havelte), Phoenix import, Danny Becher and Dick de Ruiter
Drawings: Eva Rudy Jansen
Printing and binding: Bariet, Ruinen, Holland

ISBN 978 90 78302 16 2

www.binkey-kok.com
www.altamira-becht.nl
www.diepmagazine.nl

To Amitabha
The Lord of Meditation and Intuition

CONTENTS

ACKNOWLEDGMENTS

The particular sources of the ideas, statements, and information given in this book are not always acknowledged within the text. This is not done out of a lack of respect, but simply so that the text can be read easily without too many distracting details. A complete summary of the written and verbal sources used is given at the end of the book. However, I would like to acknowledge and thank those who have been the most important sources. In their own way, they have all been my teachers, not only for this book but also on the path of my life. They are:

Joska Soos, a Hungarian shaman who lives in Antwerp, and introduced me to singing bowls ten years ago. Since then, he has continued to teach me about shamanism and the shamanistic use of sound and singing bowls. He is the only person I know who actually learned first-hand some of the secrets of the singing bowls by Tibetan monks at least until the first publication of this book. Then I met with Mr. Phuntsog Wangyal of the Tibet Foundation in London, who confirmed everything I had learned so far about the use of the bowls in ritual meditation and prayer.

I first met *Dries Langeveld*, chief editor of the magazine *BRES*, when I began to write this book. He proved to be an exceptional teacher in this field. He has made available to me his extensive knowledge of the origins, background, and use of singing bowls, has shared his own ideas on singing bowls, and taught me some special applications and ways of using them.

Hans de Back is a sound therapist, friend, and colleague in sound and story telling. He passed his knowledge and experience of singing bowls and tingshaws to me.

Danny Becher and Lisa Borstlap set up the Institute of Sound and Form together and did many years of research into the connection between the two. They allowed me to make use of their vast knowledge of the therapeutic uses of singing bowls and the wonderful world of vibrations.

Erik Bruijn, a writer, traveler in Tibet, and expert on Buddhism, enthusiastically allowed me to use a passage from his book *Tantra, Yoga and Meditation.*

The publishing company *Sirius and Siderius* generously gave me permission to use the wonderful story about "The Master in Sound" told by the explorer Alexandra David-Neel in her book *Tibet, Land of Bandits, Priests and Demons.*

Margot Kool and Koosje van der Kolk, of the Tibetan Buddhist Study and Meditation center Maitreya Institute (Gelugpa tradition) shared important knowledge about function and use of the Tibetan bell with me.

Lama Gawang of the Tibetan-Buddhist center Karma Deleg Chöhpel Ling (Kagyu tradition) took me beyond knowledge and showed me the true meaning of the Lama's use of bell and dorje: tab-sherab.

Finally, *Binkey Kok,* a lover of singing bowls, who also imports them from Tibet, got me fired up with his enthusiasm and gave me the opportunity to experiment in his warehouse so that I could find out and experience for myself everything that I had learned from others.

All my teachers agreed on this particular point: you can always talk about sound but in the end it is one's own personal experience of sound that is the real way—first to the sound itself and from there into the inner being. Where, in the heart of the labyrinth, there are many, many worlds to be found and you can recognize them all if you learn to differentiate between the different sounds of a singing bowl—if you listen closely!

INTRODUCTION

••••••

A journey of a thousand miles begins with a single step.

Lao Tse, *Tao Te Ching*

The large metal bowl sits heavily in my hand. I strike the rim gently with a felt-tipped beater. A humming, singing sound envelops me. The deep, throbbing undertones gradually change into undulating overtones. I strike the bowl again and then again and again. The more I strike, the more the room in which I am sitting is filled with sound. The sound calms me. I gradually lose an awareness of time and place. I am living in the sound and the sound is living in me.

The singing bowl sound is affecting more and more people in the same way. The phenomenon of the singing bowl (or "Tibetan bells," as they are also sometimes called) is becoming increasingly well known. The wonderful singing sounds of these bowls are being discovered by more people through concerts and through the tapes and records that have been produced, and many people would like to develop their interest by acquiring one of these bowls themselves.

With an increasing awareness of the sound of the singing bowl comes the mystery of where the sound originates and what is its true purpose. The few people who really know something about Tibetan singing bowls all have different views. Some have worked with the bowls for many years, some have traveled the border states of the Himalayas, while others have made detailed studies of the origin of these unique sounds. On some points there is agreement; on others, opinions differ totally. What is an unsuspecting amateur of the singing bowl, fascinated by the sound and curious about its origin and use, to make of this?

After months of study, investigation, and discussion with the few experts that I could find in the Netherlands, I have come to one definite conclusion: everyone should decide for him- or herself. The experience of the sound itself is and will always be the most important factor. In this book I bring together different views on singing bowls, but, there are bound to be some loose ends I've missed. In addition, I will explain the phenomenon of sound in greater depth—both its effect in general, and the effect of the sounds of singing bowls in particular.

People often think that the physical and spiritual effects of singing bowls are a matter of suggestion, or that you must in some way believe in them in order to experience their influences, yet no one would suggest that you have to believe in music in order to hear it. Sound is a physical phenomenon, and the perception of sound takes place in accordance with principles that can be explained in physical and biological terms. That means it is possible to describe exactly how sound works, why it is the way it is, and how it produces its particular effects. These natural laws are, in fact, the secret that lies behind everything and that every religion tries to explain. It is striking that the various explanations often use similar fundamental principles, sometimes corroborated by recent scientific discoveries.

Nevertheless, even the laws of nature have a secret core. Secrets guard themselves well and eventually only reveal themselves to people who are prepared to find their own way through the labyrinth of phenomena and explanations. The path they follow will only lead to an understanding of the mystery through their own experience and intuition.

I do not claim that this book gives a complete picture, or that it is in some way the ultimate truth. At best, it is a summary of opinions, ideas, and phenomena. However, I do hope that it will serve as a reader's guide—especially the part of the book that deals with the practical aspects of finding a singing bowl for you and getting to know it better.

The information on the use of sound in meditation, healing, and prayer is completed by the addition of a chapter about the character and purpose of tingshaws, Tibetan bells, and dorje.

Eva Rudy Jansen

Eighth expanded edition

I am thrilled to add these words to our eighth expanded and completely revised edition—it means the book meets the obvious need for meaningful and useful information, now updated to provide the latest information. We sincerely hope that this edition will find its way to a large and interested audience.

Dick de Ruiter

Part 1
GETTING ACQUAINTED

•••••••

There is nothing in the world that does not speak to us.
Everything and everybody reveals their own nature,
character, and secrets continuously. The more we open
up our inner senses, the more we can understand the
voice of everything.

Hazrat Inayat Khan, *Music and Mysticism*

1 The Meeting of East and West

Before the beginning of this century, travel abroad was the privilege of merchants, soldiers, missionaries, anthropologists, and the rich in search of adventure, in roughly that order. They would return home with reports that were colored by their own view of the world. Thus, for many years, people who lived in foreign lands were usually described as "barbarians, savages, heathens" and their views on life, their philosophies, and religions were often labeled as "superstitious," "idolatrous" and sometimes even "childish." However, there were some travelers who learned to respect the beliefs of the cultures they visited. Some travelers, such as the Frenchwoman Alexandra David-Neel, who became a Buddhist, even adopted such beliefs as the guiding principles of their own lives. However, people like this were the exception rather than the rule.

In the 1960s a fundamental change took place. A new youth culture spread from California throughout the Western world in the form of the hippie movement, advocating "flower power," spiritual growth, peace on earth, and a new way for people to live together. With characters such as the Beatles leading the way, people began to turn their attention to the East and even traveled there. They went east not with a bag full of money and looking for material wealth, but hitchhiking, and in search of new spiritual values.

East and West came together in the ashrams of India and the mountains of Nepal. This time, the Eastern people were the teachers and the Westerners were the humble, curious students. They realized they had not only found new ways of thinking and new spiritual paths, but had also stumbled upon an unknown world of sound. It is possible that the significance and application of sound, which were still common knowledge in the East, were once known about in the West, but were either completely destroyed in Europe during the Druids' time (or died with the indigenous peoples of the Americas) or, in modem times have been overshadowed by the inflexible rules of rational thinking. One of the "sound phenomena" that the spiritual tourists discovered south of the Himalayas, and that later gradually appeared in Europe and the United States, was the singing bowl. These were round, metal bowls of various sizes, some polished, some with a matte finish, or a golden, or occasionally almost black color. They always produce a wonderful singing sound when they are tapped, struck, or rubbed. Many people would experience this sound in the same way that Binkey Kok describes:

> I have traveled to the Far East regularly for the past twenty years. About ten or twelve years ago I saw a bronze bowl that was being sold by a Tibetan from whom I occasionally bought jewelry. I asked him what it was. He said it was a singing bowl, and that was the first time I had ever heard of such a thing. He tapped the bowl with his fingernail, and I heard a familiar and at the same time, quite unfamiliar sound. I was hooked. I wanted a bowl like this. The Tibetan was not prepared to sell his bowl, but a day or two later he had another bowl for me. He refused to tell me where it came from. As soon as you start to make inquiries, you are told that the bowls are just dishes for eating or household articles.

The fact that it was a Tibetan who sold the bowl could just be chance. I have never heard of anyone else who has either heard or bought a singing bowl in Tibet. That does not mean that they do not exist in Tibet. The Tibetan merchant who sold the bowl could just as well be a sign that singing bowls do also actually come from Tibet. If this is the case, they would have appeared in the West as a result of the Chinese invasion of Tibet in 1951. Initially, the Chinese left the lamas and their monasteries more or less alone. But then they systematically began to destroy the monasteries and thousands of Tibetan monks died, while most of the survivors fled the country. It is said that more than ninety percent of the Tibetan monasteries and temples were razed to the ground.

The monks obviously could not carry much with them when they fled from the Chinese and later, in dire poverty, they were forced to sell some of the possessions that they had managed to take out of Tibet. In this way the religious artifacts of the lamas appeared on the market stalls of Nepal and Northern India. It is possible that the bowls that are now known in the West as singing bowls were amongst these belongings. The question as to whether or not these bowls were originally singing bowls will be discussed later in this book. Joska Soos's experience seems to prove that they are, in fact, the originals. In the early 1980s he went to a lama monastery in England for an extended retreat. The lamas he met listened to him, studied his horoscope, and advised him that he should become involved with sound if he wished to accelerate his spiritual development.

> They took me to a small room and there were the bowls. I listened to them. Afterwards they presented me with some bowls. I did not have to go on a retreat. I merely had to intensify my path, immersing myself in the sounds. I did this very attentively, without forcing myself. Slowly it came to me, the whole universe opened up. Amongst the lamas themselves, these bowls are used only in secret rituals by . . . acknowledged masters in sound. They have learned to sing the ritual songs and play the ritual instruments correctly. They use the singing bowls in secret and only for themselves, not in public, and not even for other monks. It is strictly forbidden to talk about the rituals or the singing bowls themselves. This is because a knowledge of sound carries with it great power. It allows one to travel without moving. It is possible to come into contact with planets and their spirits, with the subterranean kingdom of Aggartha and with Shamballah, the earthly center of the Immortals. If you ask a lama with a singing bowl in his hands, whether it is true that they are used for psychic, psychological, and physical purposes, he will smile and reply, "Perhaps."

2 Masters of Sound

Secrets keep themselves. If Joska Soos's experience is not an iso-lated one, if there are "masters of sound" working with singing bowls behind closed doors in other Tibetan monasteries, they have certainly kept their secret well, at least as regards the singing bowls. With regard to the mastery of sound, there are testimonies from other witnesses. For example, in his book, *Tantra, Yoga and Meditation, the Tibetan way to Enlightenment,* Erik Bruijn describes the symbolic composition of the Tibetan temple orchestra in the following way:

> ...The sounds produced by the musical instruments form the counterpart to the inner sounds that can be observed in the body in a state of total stillness. If one shuts out the sounds from the outside world, one can hear the murmur of the circulation of the blood, and after a while, also the rhythm of one's own heartbeat. Because they are able to direct their concentration inwards for a long time, experi-enced monks and yogis are able to clearly detect the most subtle vibrations generated by organic processes in their own bodies. The characteristics of the sounds they hear are described with great accuracy in Tibetan aesthetics on music. These texts describe singing, beating, thumping, clashing, tinkling, complaining, and blaring sounds. The musical sounds that serve as the counterpart to these or-ganic sounds are produced by the instruments, which constitute the temple orchestra. The "rustling" is repre-sented by the sound of the conch, the "beating" is pro-duced by hand drums, the "thumping" by the big drums, the "clanging" by cymbals, the "tinkling" by bells and the "groaning" by the sound of the shepherd's pipes...

In 1983, a group of Dutch artists and musicians co-operated to-gether on a project in which body sounds—such as the heartbeat and the circulation of the blood—were amplified and reproduced as a theatrical piece. This was presented as "an audible journey through the body." Erik, who attended this performance, noted how accurately the Tibetan monks reproduced the body's sounds. He comments, "What I heard was precisely the sound of the Tibetan temple orchestra."

Alexandra David-Neel describes another wonderful experience with sound in her book Tibet, Bandits, Priests and Demons, When she entered the temple in the Bön monastery of Tesmon, the service that was being conducted was rudely interrupted. While a lama was busy with a *kyilkhor*, a magic diagram, and sacred cakes, called *formas*, one of her bearers entered the temple, clearly indicating that he was not very impressed by the sacred rituals. He was ordered away by the monks. Objecting and cursing violently, he insulted the lamas by shouting out that the tormas were only made of *momo* dough (bread dough).

> ...Then, as the man came forward, the *bönpo*[1] grasped a *chang*,[2] which was standing next to him, and swung it around. Strange, savage sounds filled the room with a tidal wave of vibrations that pierced my ears. The disrespectful peasant screamed and staggered back with his arms held up as though he was warding off something threatening.
>
> "Get out," the lama repeated again.
> The other bearers grabbed their friend and rushed out of the temple, greatly disturbed.
> Bong! Bong! continued the drum. The accompanying *bönpo* returned unperturbed, sat in front of the *kyilkhor*, and continued the muffled singing and chanting.
> What had happened? I hadn't noticed anything, except for that extraordinary sound. I went outside and asked my bearers. The troublemaker who had disturbed the sacred ritual had lost his bravado.
> "It was a snake. I tell you," he said, nodding to the others who sat around him. "A snake of fire came out of the *chang*."
> "What? Did you really see a snake of fire?" I asked. "Is that why you recoiled?"

"Didn't you see it?" they replied. "It came out of the *chang* when the lama beat upon it."

"You must have dreamt it," I said. "I didn't see anything."

"We didn't see the snake, but we did see flashes of light shoot out of the *chang*," the other bearers interjected.

In fact, they had all been witnesses to a miracle. Only I, an unworthy foreigner, had been blind.

The writer decided to apologize to the lama, and he accepted her apology amicably.

...The obligations of politeness had been fulfilled. The *bönpo* remained silent. I had to leave but I was still intrigued by the bizarre sound I had heard and the extraordinary vision the villagers had seen. Inadvertently, I looked at the *chang* that had been the start of this whole phantasmagoria. The lama read my thoughts easily. "Would you like to hear the sound again?" he asked, with a rather mocking smile.

"Yes, Kouchog, I would very much like to, if you have no objections. The instrument has a quite remarkable sound. Would you mind letting me hear it again?"

"You can play it yourself," he replied, and handed me the *chang*.

"I haven't had any practice," I told him. Certainly, the sound I produced sounded nothing like the sound I had heard. "I do not have your skill, Kouchog," I said to the lama as I gave the instrument back to him. "No snakes of fire came out of your *chang*."

The *bönpo* looked at me questioningly. Was he pretending not to understand or did he actually not understand?

"Yes," I continued, "the rude man who shouted at you claims that he saw a snake of fire coming out of the *chang* that was trying to swoop down on him. The others with him saw either flashes of light or sparks."

"That is the power of the *zoung*[8] that I cast," declared the lama emphatically. Speaking more softly he said: "The sound creates shapes and beings . . . the sound inspires them."

I think he was quoting from a text. I remarked that the people from India, the *tchirolpa*,[4] also made such claims.

I hoped that by saying this, I would encourage him to explain his point of view and to speak about the religious path that he followed, and I went on: "However, some people believe that the power of thought transcends that of sound,"

"There are also lamas who believe that," answered the *bönpo*. "Everyone has his own point of view. Ways of working differ. I am a master of sound. Through sound I can kill what lives and bring back to life what is dead..."

"Kouchog, these two things, life and death, do they really exist as opposites, completely different from each other?"

"Are you a *Dzogtchenpa*?"[5] asked the man opposite me.

"One of my teachers was a *Dzogtchenpa*," I replied evasively.

The *bönpo* then fell silent. I wanted to bring the conversation back to the question of life and death and to find out what his theories on the subject were, but his silence was not very encouraging. Should I interpret it as a polite way of showing me that it was time I left?

But then the lama mumbled something indistinctly, took hold of the *chang* and made it ring a few times.

It was wonderful! Instead of hearing the terrifying sound he had made earlier or the rather disharmonious sounds I had produced myself, I heard a melodious carillon of silver bells. How was that possible? Was this *bönpo* simply an artist who had withdrawn from the world, and could anyone, given enough practice, achieve such different effects on such a primitive instrument as the *chang*, or must I accept that he was a "master of sound" as he so proudly declared? My desire to continue the conversation with the lama increased. Would I succeed in getting him to explain to me the mystery of the *chang*?

Unfortunately for Alexandra the conversation was broken off at that point, and she was only able to continue the next day when she invited the lama to have tea with her. The conversation began with polite inquiries from the lama about India.

...I controlled myself and tried to satisfy his curiosity, hoping that I would have an opportunity to ask questions myself. The opportunity arose when he spoke about the *doubthobs*[6] of India.

"It isn't necessary to go to India to meet people with these powers," I said to him.

"I believe that you yourself proved that to me yesterday evening. The Hindus also revere Tibet as a sanctuary of great and wise men, and they believe that the magicians who live in Tibet are more powerful than their own magicians."

"That is possible," replied the *bönpo*. "I have never been to India. You're thinking about the *chang*, aren't you? Why do you attach such importance to something so trivial? Sound has other mysteries.

Sound is produced by all beings and all things, even those which appear to have no soul. Every being and thing has its own sound, but this sound changes depending upon on the state of the being or thing producing the sound at any particular moment. How does that work? Everything is a collection of atoms (*rdul phra*) which dance and produce sounds by their movements.

It is said that in the beginning the wind created the *gyatams*,[7] the basis of our world, by a spinning movement. This movement of the wind was melodious and it was this kind of sound that combined the form and the matter of the *gyatam*[8] to form a whole. The first *gyatams* sang, and from them emerged shapes that, in turn, produced others through the power of the sound that they had made. This applies not only to the past but is still true today. Every atom ceaselessly sings its song, constantly creating coarse and fine substances. And just as there are creative sounds, there are also destructive sounds which cause matter to disintegrate. Anyone who can produce both sounds can create and destroy at will. In fact, a *doubthob* who can produce the basic destructive sound which lies at the root of all destructive sounds,[9] should be able to wipe out this world and all the worlds of the gods, up to the world of the mighty 'Thirty-three' of which the Buddhists speak."

After this explanation he said goodbye, expressing the wish that the following day would be fine and that I should have a successful journey. His explanation of this rather doubtful theory was certainly interesting, but it did not, in any way, clarify what I called the "mystery of the *chang.*"

Alexandra David-Neel found these theories obscure, but the lama's story has been told in different ways all over the world, and his explanation about moving atoms creating sounds comes surprisingly close to the theories of modern atomic physics.

Part 2

HISTORY

· · · · · · ·

"Don't you think so, Pooh?"
"Don't I think what?" said Pooh, as he opened his eyes.
"Music and life..."
"Amount to the same thing," said Pooh.

Benjamin Hoff, *The Tao of Pooh*

3 The Origin of Things

The concept of sound as a medium that can transport the human spirit to a different state of consciousness is as old as humanity itself. It is a concept that can be observed everywhere, all the time, not only in humans but also in animals. Wordless sounds transmit messages that are accompanied by states ranging from tension to relaxation, uneasiness to a sense of well-being. Animals can attract each other or scare each other off, reassure or warn each other with sounds. We are no different. Every mother is familiar with the communication between her and her newborn baby. She responds immediately to the baby's crying and her soft crooning lulls the baby to sleep.

This is not a "discovery"; it is a fact of nature that can be utilized by anyone who has the ability to produce sound.

What might be indeed considered a discovery, is that some people, as well as some animals, can produce sounds using things other than vocal chords. To begin with, the body produces many other sounds: heartbeat, circulation, digestion. Objects outside the body can also make sounds, either independently or when people use them. They can be dropped, shaken, struck, blown into, or rubbed together. Each of these sounds has a specific effect; they can give you goose bumps, or just a pleasant feeling. They conjure up feelings and images.

In creation myths all over the world, sound is recognized as the source of all visible and invisible things. The sound is preserved in those things. Just as all created things have their own sound, they also sing their own song. The lama's explanation in Alexandra David-Neel's story is a clear example of this.

The realization that man is a part of this whole, and the search to stay in touch with this whole, was already being expressed in early cultures through the use of sound. This can be found in Shamanism, which is probably the oldest existing religion on earth. Shamanism itself is actually already removed from the fundamental principle that every man has perfect communication with himself and his surroundings, as well as with the supernatural. After all, the shaman is still capable of this communication, which others can no longer achieve by themselves. And a shaman can restore communication when it has been temporarily disturbed. To achieve this, the shaman makes intensive use of sound, primarily with a drum and his voice, but also with rattles and wind instruments. Joska Soos mentioned as the first of the Six Shamanistic Axioms: "Sound is the basic element." Before the shaman took over this function, thus isolating it out of the whole range of possibilities at man's disposal, every member of the group (clan, tribe) played an equal part in the ritual. Later, the shaman, medicine man, or magician became the leader in these rituals. The aim was to allow everyone to experience his existence, to express his feelings, and to take his place as a link in the chain that connects from the first mythical beings, through his ancestors into the next generation. Through song, dance, and drumming, he interrelated with the place where he was, the community, and the natural world around him. He made contact with his own inner space, with its contents, and with visible and invisible space outside himself. He placated gods, demons, forefathers, and natural spirits. He gathered his strength together and expressed his eroticism.

In fact, we still speak of "tuning in," to indicate that we wish to establish an intense form of communication. And if this communication does not happen, there is no "sound" connection. People who seemed to have a definite talent in establishing this delicately tuned relationship (to the gods, for example) began to perform special tasks. In addition to attending the daily duties, such a gifted individual went on to become a leader, shaman, or jester. Later, the people who fulfilled these functions were gradually relieved of their daily work so that they could dedicate themselves wholly to their special tasks. In this way they became important, "chosen," and the priesthood was a natural next step. Consequently they became specially consecrated priests, who had to study for many years, sometimes had to undergo many tests, and often deliberately isolated themselves from daily life, to act as negotiators. The priest was no longer an ordinary person among other people, but became someone placed outside and above others, with the sole right to represent God on Earth when necessary, and even assume that identity.

Just as there have always been discoverers who traveled around the world to see it with their own eyes, there have always been people who only try to follow their own perceptions and constantly strive to establish their own links between the inner and outer worlds. Many of them were burnt as heretics or put to death in other ways.

We now live in an age called the "Age of Aquarius," which is characterized by a great wish to be freed from all tyranny. More and more people recognize that they themselves are responsible. They will not, anxiously or obediently, let external circumstances be imposed on them from above. They are seeking an inner communication with the worlds in and around them, with the "Cosmos," a commonly used term. They no longer need the intervention of the priest, doctor, or doctor-priest: the shaman. This is why there is so much interest in the different ways and means by which we can re-establish inner communication. That is why there is increasing interest in the fundamental way of achieving this through sound.

4 Of Ringing Stones and Fountain Bowls

In Asia, the use of sounding objects is very old. For example, the Chinese Emperors had the right to the most beautiful ringing stones—hard stones, such as jade, which produce a ringing sound when they are struck. The first great emperors reigned from about 2000 B.C.E. There are records of a Bronze Age culture in China in about 1600 B.C.E., and archeological finds in northeast Thailand suggest that bronze was already used there about two thousand years earlier. Such finds show only that bronze articles were made that long ago, but until even older objects are found, it is impossible to say how much further back in history bronze was being worked. It is clear that by the sixth century B.C.E. the Chinese were far advanced in the manufacture of metal alloys and in the working of metals, from which they made perfectly tuned bells. It is difficult to say how many of these bells were made before that time, until earlier finds can tell us more. It is obvious that no culture can suddenly, from one day to the next, produce a tuned bell that weighs more than one hundred pounds, let alone a bell that can produce two different pure tones, depending on where it is struck. There must be some previous history. The study of sound and the effects of vibrations was so advanced in the fifth century B.C.E. that so-called "fountain bowls" were made from that time. These are bronze bowls with very specific shapes and dimensions. When such a bowl is filled with the correct amount of water, and the handles attached to the side of the bowl are rubbed in a special way with the palm of the hand, a fountain of water rises up, and a humming sound is produced.

Bowls are still used in Japan, for example, as standing temple bells without clappers. They are made of a black metal alloy and produce a short, rather dry sound. The singing sound of various metal alloys has been extensively used in the many different gongs found in Asia. The discovery that metal objects produce sounds was made all over the world, and certainly small, metal, skull-shaped bowls were known around 1100 B.C.E. With these bowls, you can strike the forehead by the nasal bone and the point of the temple on the edge of the bowl to produce two distinct tones with an interval of exactly a major third apart. That is by no means a coincidence. In the art of singing harmonics (i.e., producing a higher note above a particular basic note by using different resonant cavities in the head and body), it has been shown that the interval of a third remains the same. The makers of skull bowls had already discovered that this is the result of the shape of the skull; the distance between the nasal bone and the temple bone produces a major third. These bowls are the oldest known objects that can be described as "singing bowls."

5 Singing Bowls, Chalices, Food Dishes

Most singing bowls do not originate from Tibet, but from Nepal or India. In addition, we now know of singing bowls from other countries, such as China and Japan, and more recently, the singing bowls made of quartz crystal from the United States (see chapter 25). The caravan routes of Asia not only transported goods for trade, but also served to spread knowledge and religion. Shamans traveled south via Mongolia, and Buddhism crossed the Himalayas from India to the north. Shamanism and Buddhism came together in Tibet. The original religion of Tibet was the shamanistic-animistic Bon religion. In the seventh century C.E. the famous King Srongtsen (or Srong Btsan) Gampo married two princesses, one from Nepal, and the other from China. Both women were devout Buddhists. Gradually, two new movements developed: Lamaism, which is essentially Buddhist, but reveals strong Bön influences, and the Bön religion, which is now a sort of shamanistic branch of Buddhism.

Both branches of Tibetan Buddhism make intensive use of sound in their rituals and meditations (see Part 1).

But if you ask a traveler in the Himalayas if he has ever heard singing bowls in a monastery, or if you ask a Tibetan if the bowls we know as singing bowls are, or were ever used as singing bowls, the answer is nearly always negative.

There are round metal bowls in photographs of temple interiors, and they look exactly like our singing bowls; but clearly they are used as chalices. Travelers return from Nepal with accounts of metal bowls with a golden color, which are used for eating.

But if they are only offertory dishes and eating bowls, why the sound? And who made them like that? There are various opinions about who made the singing bowls, but they all point back to the shamanistic tradition.

In the first place, there are accounts of traveling smiths that also date back to this tradition.

But did these metal smiths make the bowls on their own initiative, or were they commissioned to make the bowls? Were the customers monks who had the required knowledge to determine the proportion of different metals for the desired result? The metal alloys must have been made using a very special process which modern techniques are still unable to reproduce. There is also a theory that the monks themselves were the metal workers who made the bowls. But then why do the people of Nepal use them for eating? No one has ever seen the bowls made in the old way, either by lamas or by traveling metal smiths. Bowls are still made nowadays, but they are cast, and the old alloys are no longer used.

According to tradition, the bowls are made of seven metals—one metal for each of the planets:

gold	the Sun
silver	the Moon
mercury	Mercury
copper	Venus
iron	Mars
tin	Jupiter
lead	Saturn

All these metals produce an individual sound, including harmonics, and together these sounds produce the exceptional singing sound of the bowl. The actual proportions of the different metals vary in each bowl, and it seems that not all bowls are made of all seven metals. Sometimes more metals are used, sometimes fewer. Thus the true Tibetan bowl is said to be made with more silver and tin, giving it a dull, anthracite luster, while Nepalese bowls have the familiar golden glow.

However, the explanation for the differences in composition could also be that the travelling metal smiths did not carry their raw materials with them, but used the ores available in a particular area, which often contained several different metals.

The mountains and plateaus of the "roof of the world" are

richer in metal ores than in clay. That is why eating utensils were made mainly of metal or wood for a long time.

We can only try to reconstruct the method used to make a bowl from the original alloy, but it was probably as follows: the liquid metal was poured out onto a flat stone and left to cool as a metal plate. Then this plate was beaten with a hammer into the shape of a bowl, of which the metal was under maximum tension without cracking.

The inscriptions, decorations and other patterns that sometimes decorate the metal, were then punched into it. Mostly, these are markings in Tibetan script, for instance the name of the original owner. Probably, the customer could order a bowl from traveling smiths, with a specific sound or other quality.

There would be a number of bowls, all of which would have roughly the same sound, but with slight differences in the balance of sound and the harmonics. The customer would make a choice from the bowls that were all of good quality. This could explain why there are still so many bowls in circulation, even though they have not been made in the traditional way for the last forty years.

Another explanation is that many singing bowls were sacrificial dishes, and these were always very common in Tibetan monasteries. The fact that they have a special sound is because a gift offered in a sacrificial dish must also be harmonious in every respect. Therefore dishes must have a pure sound even though they are never rung out loud.

This does not mean that bowls were not also used as eating dishes. It is possible that the alloys of the bowls supplied homeopathic potencies of essential minerals in the diet. For example, a woman who had just had a baby would eat from these bowls for a whole month. But, if the bowls were really made by nomadic metal smiths/shamans, and if they were used in monasteries behind closed doors, then there are good reasons for everyone to keep silent about their shamanistic singing use, and to answer queries with "I don't know," or dismiss them as "eating bowls." Buddhism is the dominant religion in the Himalayas, where these bowls are found. Singing bowls are not used in "official" Buddhist rituals. No one will openly admit that they own these objects that imply the practice of shamanistic rituals. For centuries, even people in Christian countries have had to hide the fact that they are still using pre-Christian rituals. But everyone needs dishes to eat from, so you could always buy them openly and display them in your home, ready to be used. No matter what they were used for.

There could be many reasons why these bowls have not been made for the past forty years in the way described. An eating dish made of metal is very difficult to clean. So where the dishes were actually used for this purpose they have been replaced by porcelain and earthenware imported from China. If the dishes were used for sacrificial rituals, the Chinese invasion of Tibet was the reason. With so many monasteries being destroyed, the demand for sacrificial dishes suddenly and dramatically ended. Thus there is no longer such a need for new bowls. The existing bowls can meet the present demand. But with increasing exports, especially to the United States, the question arises how long that will continue. If there were to be a greater demand for new bowls (and the more Western traders discover the bowls, the more there will be a commercial demand for new supplies from the local traders) they would no longer be made in the traditional way. The nomadic smiths seem to have disappeared. The knowledge handed down to them is dying out with them.

6 Ancient and Newly Made

The lack of information about the origin of the singing bowls is also due to the Chinese occupation of Tibet, beginning in 1949. In just a couple of years, the age-old religious heritage, knowledge, and wisdom was nearly wiped out, while public religious practice was prohibited. Although almost immediately a huge stream of refugees crossed the high mountains of the Himalayas toward northern India—to a place called "Little Tibet," with Dharamshala as a residence-in-exile of the Dalai Lama—these people were not able to take their temple treasures with them. A lot of these were buried in secret places; some of them still are. According to traditional standards, there have been two renowned places in Tibet where these singing bowls were authentically forged and hammered, but these were also shut down after the Chinese invasion. Since then, these kinds of singing bowls are no longer made. Maybe there still are some very old monks who know some details of this age-old craft, but if there is not a very thorough investigation by scientists soon—with approval from the Chinese, of course—this ancient art and knowledge will be lost forever.

American researcher Randall Gray, who has been investigating singing bowls for many years, could find only some oral legends and tales— no written documents whatsoever—about these ancient Tibetan singing bowls. According to one of these tales, in the past there were three huge Tibetan monasteries, each hosting hundreds of monks, each of which had one huge singing bowl with an enormous, far-reaching sound that could contribute to spiritual enlightenment. There were also thousands of smaller singing bowls that were played during certain ceremonies. That must have been an awesome sound!

There are very few knowledgeable people who are able to recognize authentic ancient singing bowls and their age. Mostly this age cannot be determined at all. You may wonder if this is important or not. After all, it is the sound of the singing bowl itself that matters: the sound quality, its depth, its harmonic overtones.

At present we know at least 45 different kinds of singing bowls. The expert will often be able to tell the origin of a singing bowl. Like the one we see in the picture on page 43 (top). This is an example from Tibet. The thickness of the material is often firm, and most bowls have an edge that has been forged inwardly, making the bowl sturdier. Simple decorations are also often present. Tibetan singing bowls are remarkably rich in harmonious overtones, assuming that they are undamaged, of course.

From Bengal come the wider angling shapes of singing bowls (see photo on this page), sometimes also with reinforced rims, and mostly made of a thinner metal. They are well-suited for being sounded by rubbing a stick around the edge (read chapter 21). In general, their overtones are harder to make audible than the Tibetan ones.

From Indonesia are bowls (photo on page 43, bottom) with high, vertical sides, which are still being made until today by special family clans. These have special sounds, clearly differing from the bowls from India and surrounding countries.

In Japan we often find very small, fine singing bowls, sounding like bells, smoothly finished (see top of page 44), with also a clear and straight sound, with the basic tone clearly audible and the overtones very lightly in the background. Nobody knows when these first showed up in Japan, but they have been integrated in their spiritual culture for ages, with just as many rituals that have such an important place in daily life of the rural population. Here the people have not yet been completely Westernized like the urban people. The Japanese do not manufacture these bowls in the usual way by forging and hammering, but they are using the metal lathe. There are some singing bowls being forged, but most are lathed. Because of this special fabrication process, they are always perfectly round, and they are also very expensive, even two or three times as expensive as the other singing bowls. They are being made in small family workshops, each with its own secret process and metal mixture, which has been passed down by generations. So there are

the *Taiho,* the *Nara,* the *Kiho* and the *Michiyuki* singing bowls. A very special series of tiny singing bowls from Japan are the ones with a high gold content and an extremely pure sound. These come from various workshops as well: the *Uneri, Unryu, Shaka, Kyoto, Zen, Shomyo* and the black lacquered *Shomyo.* These golden bowls of course are even more expensive; a set of five or seven will cost around $ 2,500.[10]

The Japanese (and Chinese) temple bells are something special, indeed. They have their

own unique sound and are mainly used during Zen meditation sessions. There are even temple bells measuring three feet or more in diameter. One can actually step inside these huge bells and experience the sound vibrations from within! However, the Japanese ones sound much better and more crystalline than the Chinese, but they are also much more costly. The Chinese singing bowls that are being shipped to the West do not come anymore from the mainland (People's Republic) but from Taiwan.

Also nowadays in India there are very beautiful and very pure-sounding new singing bowls being produced, in cooperation with German customers.[11] These bowls are shaped more like

soup plates, with slanting or half-round edges, often decorated with symbols or flowers. There are shiny, polished bowls containing more silver or gold, but there are also ones made of dark bronze and other copper alloys. Recently, another new bowl shape has been designed, which is in between an original singing bowl and a temple bell. Its sound is also a symbiosis of characteristic properties: while you can only sound an ordinary temple bell by striking it, these new bowls can also be rubbed like the ordinary singing bowl, and yet they produce the beautiful, round sound of a temple bell.

Crystal singing bowls have not been on the market that long. They are produced in the United States. These bowls are discussed further in chapter 25.

A rather peculiar singing bowl was rediscovered by the German Christof Grosse. In some old documents he found a description and image of such a bowl, originally from the Chinese middle ages, around 1500 C.E.. With the aid of a bell foundry he eventually managed to produce a perfect copy in bronze, resembling a reversed helmet, with two large half-round brass handles on the inner rim.[12] They come in four sizes, from 10 to 32 inches (26 to 80 cm) in diameter (10 to 100 pounds, or 4.5 to 45 kg!). By rubbing with your hands across these handles, you create a kind of deep humming tone that is still audible even at a few hundred yards, but you will not be able to tell from which direction the sound is coming. So we may presume these bowls originally had a function in communicating between villages. But Grosse also found out that when the bowls are filled with water, rubbing the handles will produce beautiful Chladni images (see page 52) in the water. Very peculiar!

Part 3

HOW SINGING BOWLS WORK

•••••••

Every atom constantly sings a song, and it is this tone which creates finer or denser forms of greater or smaller density.

Lama Govinda

7 External Characteristics

When you compare a number of singing bowls by placing them next to each other, it is obvious that they come in many different shapes and sounds. Most bowls are more or less golden in color. They are round, but the ratio of the circumference and the depth varies. There are fairly shallow, broad dishes, which are small or medium in size. There are round bowls that are deeper. There are bowls with a small base or with a broad base, and there are even bowls with a completely flat base and a small, straight side. Some bowls have a stand so that they have the shape of a chalice. They are generally quite small and are rather rare. Bowls with a so-called "bottle" base, which stands up concave in the bowl, are mainly made in India. They are fairly thin, and produce a different sound from the bowls hereafter referred to as "Himalayan bowls."

The thickness and color of the material used varies from bowl to bowl. Bowls with a shining gold color made of fairly thin material, round in shape, and fairly small are generally Japanese bowls. They often produce a clear sound, more like a bell.

The sound is determined by the shape and thickness of the material, as well as by the thickness of the rim. The color has no effect on the sound. There are some bowls with remnants of a dull black layer of varnish, usually on the outside. This layer is meant to be there and does not interfere with the sound. If you buy a matte bowl and polish it, this can influence the sound. By polishing the bowl, you remove a thin layer of the material so that the thickness of the metal is permanently altered.

There are very big, firm bowls, up to 6 kilos (!), but also small thin ones of only 10.5 ounces, or 300 grams. A singing bowl of some 12 inches (30 centimeters) in diameter may weigh about 4 pounds (1,700 grams)—of a fairly thick material—but also, a thinly walled bowl of the same diameter may weigh about 2.5 pounds (1,200 grams). Of course, thin-layered singing bowls will be much more vulnerable; if you drop it this could be the end of

it, with a dent, or worse, a crack. This happened once to my favorite bowl—I could only use it afterwards as a flowerpot...

Most bowls are decorated in some way, for example, with patterns of rings, stars, dots, or leaves. Sometimes there is an inscription on the outside. This is usually in the Devanagari script that is used in Nepal, and indicates the name of the owner. Sometimes the writing is Tibetan, and this also refers to the name of the owner or the name of the ceremony for which the bowl was used. The Devanagari inscriptions suggest that singing bowls originated in Nepal and are only known as Tibetan bowls because the Tibetan refugees in Nepal earn their living by their traditional activities, i.e., trade. They traded not only the goods they brought with them, but also articles that they found in their host country.

In any case it is probable that the bowls with Devanagari inscriptions come from Nepal.

Decorated bowls may also be so-called "calendar bowls"; for example, the decoration could be a lunar calendar or Jupiter calendar. The exact use of these calendar bowls is no longer known, but it is probable that the sound of the bowl and the movement of a few drops of water in it indicated which heavenly powers were present on that day, and which was the best day to use the bowl. Thus it would only sing its best on its own astrological day. The special knowledge and senses with which the influences of the celestial bodies can be calculated and used in all sorts of ways developed in other cultures as well as in Asia. For example, the Egyptian culture, closer to home, still presents a partly unsolved puzzle. The Celtic Druids also possessed this sort of knowledge and sensitivity. Perhaps singing bowls are a way of reviving these lost senses.

However, if you have your own singing bowl it will be difficult—maybe even impossible—to discover whether it is really a calendar bowl (apart from making a guess based on the visible signs inscribed on the bowl) and to find out what planet the calendar is associated with, and how it can be used.

Some bowls, especially those engraved with patterns of rings, stars, or leaves, may react like Chinese fountain bowls. When they are filled with water up to the engraved ring and are vibrated by striking or rubbing them, one or more fountains can rise up. If a star shape appears on the water, which then rises into a fountain from the middle, the bowl is called a "star bowl."

8 Sound Made Visible

The wonderful phenomena mentioned in the preceding pages have a clear explanation.

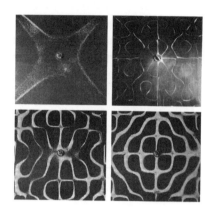

Sound is vibration, and vibration is music in a three-dimensional form. Hans Jenny has taken superb photographs of sound shapes in water. Ernst Chladni spread fine grains of sand (or iron filings) on a sheet of glass or metal, and made the sheet vibrate by stroking it with the bow of a violin. The sand instantly arranged itself into beautiful geometric patterns, rather like a mandala. When the metal sheet was stroked in a different place, a different shape was formed.

When a surface (a thin sheet of glass or metal or the surface of water) is vibrated, these vibrations spread in every direction in the same way. Because they are all produced in the same way, these waves are the same in whichever direction they spread. When two or more of these identical sound waves meet each other, they cancel each other out. The place where they meet is known as the meeting point.

The sand that lies on a vibrating sheet is shaken away by the vibrations. It collects in the places that are not vibrating—the meeting points—and in this way a pattern of lines appears. This looks like a two-dimensional pattern on the flat surface, but in reality the sound has a three-dimensional shape. The vibrations are transmitted in every direction, not just in the plane being vibrated. The three-dimensional shape of sound is visible in water. Water is a medium that can be vibrated very easily, and these vibrations travel over a large area. You can make a bowl

full of water vibrate by rubbing or beating the rim; the vibrations will then spread over the surface of the water in every direction. If the vibration becomes more intense through prolonged rubbing or a special way of striking the bowl, the vibrations meet each other in such a way that the ripples literally raise each other up. The particles sometimes rise up several inches above the surface of the water. This can result in one or more fountains of small, sparkling droplets.

9 Sound Massage

We all know the experiment at physics, when a tuning fork is struck and then put on the tabletop, causing the whole surface to resonate with its tone. Another well-known example is the stone, when thrown into the water causing expanding circles on (and below) the water surface. These experiments make us understand how sound vibrations may cause a resonance inside our bodies: all cells will reverberate. But it is of course much more complicated, when we realize that literally *every* sound and vibration around us will have this effect in the body!

For the most part, our bodies are made of water. And these body fluids are also very easily being vibrated by the sounds around us. When we then consider how many *disharmonic* sounds surround us, it is not hard to understand that the effects will not be very harmonious, especially when these sounds are lasting and loud enough. In some cases the effects will even be disastrous. And here I am not talking about the obvious cases of damaged eardrums caused by the excessive noise of airplanes, equipment, or house party music, but this is common among many of us in our daily lives: a general disturbance of the sensitive and vulnerable body balance. Of course, one person may be much more vulnerable than another, but fact is that we just cannot isolate ourselves from these sounds; they are all around us. Yes, we may plug our ears, but our body fluids will still resonate with all these sounds that are present.[13]

As already mentioned in the previous chapter, this old physics test is generally still taught at school: a metal plate covered with dry sand is resonated by a fiddlestick. Ernst Chladni, a German physicist, first demonstrated with this test how all sounds have structure. Later, this research was continued by the anthroposophist Hans Jenny, who worked with mixtures of paraffin and turpentine oil, vibrating with sinus tones, and producing very specific crystal images. The sounds made these lifeless substances turn into very specific crystal-like shapes—they were "awakened" by the sounds they were exposed to. Jenny named this natural phenomenon "cymatics."

The American researcher Barbara Hero experimented with sound frequencies, mirrors, and even laser beams, with their reflections influenced by harmonic sounds, showed beautiful, geometrically perfect images as well. In addition, she was able to demonstrate that the human voice singing harmonic overtones through her recording equipment would also create these symmetric shapes. The most appealing example thereof was the primeval Indian mantra OM, which shows a magnificent mandala, resembling significantly the age-old image of the Sri Yantra. Finally, in the last two decades, Japanese scientist Masaru Emoto took this research one step further by revealing, using resonant images on the computer, how sound affects the cell structure of living beings, and even how our thoughts can influence the energy in the cells (see bibliography).

When we perform the Chladni test with the sounds of a singing bowl, we see beautiful, harmonious patterns evolve, with resemblance to mandalas. *The sounds of these bowls work in a harmonious way!* So we may apply these sounds at certain moments when we do not feel well, out of balance, or stressed—physically as well as mentally. In my own tests with measuring equipment (including blood pressure and EEG) in the 1980s, I found that in most people *after only twenty minutes* of listening to the (recorded) sounds of singing bowls they were in a state of balance and relaxation. The effects continued for a period varying from one to four hours afterwards. In children, the effects were even stronger—they reacted sooner, but the effects were also faster gone.

Except for the body fluids, of course the other body tissues—like organs, nerves (including the brain) and also the bones—are being vibrated as well, although less than the fluid mass. There are theories that each and every body organ has its own specific frequency. This means that when, for example, you direct a sound frequency in the (midrange) pitch of G at the body, the liver, stomach, and spleen are being resonated; the pitch of C will resonate in the gall bladder and F the lungs. We can apply this practically by using the singing bowls producing these specific pitches. Of course, this is not to be practiced by amateurs; this is way too specific and we should leave this to the therapists and practitioners.

Then there is also the possibility of a direct "swaying" of the brain waves, and consequently changing our state of mind. You can read more about this in chapter 14.

With the use of singing bowls, we may even go further than resonating of sound waves inside our bodies. This phenomenon is described in chapter 11.

Sound Bath

Here we will elaborate a little more on the extraordinary practice of sound massage.

We can use singing bowls (or recordings thereof) for an extraordinary harmonization: the sound bath. This may be a very simple procedure we can do for ourselves, as described below, but the sound bath can also be utilized professionally The most ideal setting might include other therapies, like healing with herbs, massaging with aromatherapy, relaxation training, and the like.

A professional sound therapeutic practice will have at its disposal a number of singing bowls, from huge bowls and gongs to very small bells or tingshaws. However, even just three attuned singing bowls of different sizes could make a very fine and effective sound massage. And of course we can also use a good singing bowls recording,[14] using an excellent quality sound system, with loudspeakers of at least 30, but preferably 50, watts or

with surround settings so the session can literally be surrounded by sound.

By the way, not all singing bowls are suitable for use in a sound bath. If you are not familiar with this practice, please ask someone who knows. Some dealers are offering complete sound massage sets, but do not let them talk you into something you would regret later!

Choose a room with soft lighting, pastel shades, and if possible, complete silence, but in any case without disturbing, outside noises. You may decorate this room as harmoniously as possible, with perhaps one big green houseplant, some candles, with perhaps some (recorded) nature sounds, such as a calm bay, a babbling brook, or evening birds in the background. The person receiving the sound bath lies face-up on a soft mattress, or sometimes briefly on the stomach, the head supported by a small pillow. Singing bowls can be placed on top of the body on special supporting rings made of fabric, or on the floor close to the body. A place near the soles of the feet is a good area where the sound vibrations are absorbed into the body. Sometimes the one who performs the sound massage will strike a large bowl, and then move the vibrating bowl slowly over the body or around the head.

Before the sound massage begins, but also during the session, it is recommended to breathe deeply and effortlessly, with the exhalation flowing out like a sigh. Also, the person performing the session can breathe accordingly, along with the other, in harmony.

The duration of a sound bath may vary from ten (minimum) up to forty five (max) minutes.

Our imagination knows no limits with a sound massage. Imagine a chakra sound bath, with seven singing bowls tuned to the chakra tones and containing colored water in the chakra colors. With backlighting, the colored fountains from the singing bowls can be projected against a white wall. Listeners may hum along together with the chakra tones. The water in the singing bowls does not affect the pitch of the sounds, as long as it fills less than a quarter of the bowl, which is quite sufficient for the desired effect.[15]

To a certain extent, it is possible to treat yourself with a sound massage. When listening to a recording there is no limit, but when using real singing bowls, you are of course limited in the areas where you may hold the bowls. But simply striking a large bowl and moving it close to your head will give you already a wonderful—filled with wonders— sound experience!

Another special method is filling just about half of a large bowl with water and then, sitting on a chair, putting both of your feet inside the bowl. Striking it with a big felt hammer will do the trick, and will give you an extraordinary experience. This can only be done using a bowl of preferably one and a half feet in diameter.

10 Natural Harmonics and Overtones

In whatever way the people in the Himalayas may have used the bowls, one thing is certain: Western people are often affected in a special way when they first come across the sound of the singing bowl. Does this mean we cannot satisfy our desire for sound with the wealth of sound in our Western culture? Or should we ask: what is the difference, ultimately, between the sounds produced by the singing bowls and the sounds of our own musical tradition?

Music is not a chance phenomenon. Quite the reverse: everything can ultimately be traced back to music. The whole universe and everything that takes place in it consists of parts that relate to each other in the way of musical harmony. In other words: of all the theoretically possible connections and correlation that exist, the smallest known parts, as well as the largest visible parts, always choose proportions and connections that correspond to the intervals audible in music. Even these intervals are not chosen at random—of all the theoretically possible notes, the ones that are chosen have a particular ratio. For instance, if you vibrate a single string on a sounding board, and then slide your finger along the string to gradually shorten the part vibrating freely, it should be possible, in theory, to hear the pitch going up. Actually the notes that are heard always change at regular set intervals. In other words, the whole universe, everything in nature, arranges itself in musical proportions the way music itself does.

When a string is vibrated, it will produce its own basic tone, but above all it will produce a whole scale of resonating harmonics that include all the whole tones and semitones with ever-decreasing intervals. In Western music far less attention is paid to these harmonics than in the East. Bells, gongs, cymbals, as well as the bowls that come from Asia, produce far more harmonics than the musical instruments we use in the West.

Series of harmonics resonate at the natural intervals found throughout nature. They do not always sound harmonious to us. In music based in the simultaneous sounding of different basic notes (chords), Western Europeans use a system based on octaves—groups of eight tones beginning and ending with the same tone. With two successive C-natural notes, for example, the frequency (speed of vibration) of the higher note is exactly twice that of the lower note at the beginning of the octave. They sound similar, and this applies for all the other notes—D, E, F, G, A and B—and their semitones.

The most harmonious interval to our ears is a fifth, which is two notes that are five notes apart. There is a perfect fifth, which has an interval of three whole notes and one semi tone, and a diminished fifth, which comprises an interval of two whole tones and two semitones. Beginning on a C and progressing in perfect fifths, it takes twelve fifths before you strike another C note. This cycle of twelve fifths is called "a circle of fifths." In a circle of fifths there are eight Cs, including the first and last C. This means that the circle consists of seven octaves. However, if you calculate the frequency in numbers, you find that seven ascending octaves have a frequency of 128 together, while twelve ascending circles of fifths (there is a difference of 1.5 in the frequency of the lowest and highest note in a fifth) together have a frequency number of 129.75. So much for your perfect intervals! In the 16th century, a Chinese prince found the following solution: when instruments were tuned, the intervals were artificially shortened. A century later, J.S. Bach wrote *Das Wohltemperierte Klavier* ("The Well-Tempered Clavier"), the first long, European composition that was based on this new principle of so-called even temperature.

Since then we have only heard music in which all the intervals are just too short in relation to their natural wavelength. Rational thinking has placed restraint on sound.

Gongs and singing bowls break through these artificial barriers. The natural vibration of the intervals between the harmony can be clearly heard. They sound different. They affect us differently. Sometimes free-floating sounds are experienced as unharmonious to the Western ear. In fact, it would be more accurate to describe them as "multi-harmonious." The sound comprises more subtle distinctions than you can hear in the calculated intervals of the well-tempered octave.

11 Harmonic Overtones

Singing bowls are par excellence instruments for demonstrating and practicing the healing effects of harmonic overtones. The physical phenomenon of resonance (see chapter 9) causes the harmonizing sounds of a good singing bowl to resonate harmonically within the body—in the body fluids, the entire nerve system, brains included, in all of our organs and tissues, even in our bone structure.

Of course not all singing bowls are equally suitable for this purpose. Not every singing bowl has strong and audible harmonic overtones, and the singing bowl needs to be perfectly round and most of all big enough to vibrate the air around the body, which in turn will resonate our body. Smaller singing bowls are only usable for sound therapy on the head. In some rare singing bowls you can hear no less than seven harmonic overtones! With a special rubbing technique, some of these

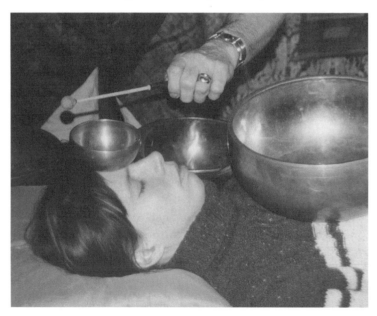

overtones can be accentuated, so they may even sound louder than the basic tone.

Our average hearing will be able to perceive a number of overtones consciously—with a good hearing up to about 16,000 hertz (or cps, cycles per second, also written as Hz)—but with sensitive equipment it has been established that on top of this, in the very high sound frequencies, harmonic overtones will continue up to 22,000 Hz, far beyond our hearing ability. One of the peculiar discoveries in this high frequency research has been that even if we cannot hear these tones, apparently we perceive them as the "coloring" of sounds. When we remove these high frequencies from a sound recording, the sounds or music become dull and cold, like something is missing. Well, there is, literally, something missing![16] But what is more, the French physician Alfred Tomatis, founder of Audio-Psycho-Phonology, discovered that these high frequencies are indeed somehow received by our hearing, and are transformed and stored as physical and mental energy. In sound therapy sessions, the patient will listen to music that has been filtered, with extra emphasis on these higher frequencies; that is why the listening equipment of this therapy must be high quality. As a result, the listener will become much more energetic and mentally clear. Another effect of this sound therapy is—as a result of special manipulations in the music—the restorative effects on the inner ear: hearing impairments such as some forms of deafness and tinnitus may be healed or improved.

The very high frequencies are also part of the harmonic overtones of the singing bowls; as such, these overtones have a healing effect on both our hearing and our life energy.

The use of sung overtones, together with the sounds of the singing bowls, will be discussed further in the practical part of this book, chapter 18. First, we will make a little detour to the human voice.

12 Holy Wholesome Singing

Overtones are part of our own voices as well. In the middle of the last century, when sound technique was still in its infancy, recorded music and voices did not sound very realistic, because not all of the frequencies could be stored and transferred. Nowadays, these techniques have been refined to such an extent that the sound is conceived as full and warm; this is partly as a result of being able to capture these higher frequencies.

When we listen to a singer's performance, his or her ability to produce an easy range of harmonic vocal overtones will influence our appreciation, whether we like it or not. Of course, there are other factors, such as expression, meaning what they are singing, and condition of the voice, but listen carefully next time you hear a famous singer—how rich the overtones are in such a voice!

Harmonic overtones work literally in healing: making whole. They have a direct effect on mind and body; most people are able to notice this. Sound has a natural attraction on us. Most people, especially children, and even animals love listening to music. Of course there will always be differences in taste, but this natural attraction is always there. With rhythmic music we get the natural urge to move our bodies and dance. With relaxing music we feel the boon in our muscles and in our mind. Also, expression through our own voices is such an international phenomenon that boundaries may be crossed and disputes may be settled.

In our era, when we are being overwhelmed by so many impressions through the media, the busy world around us and the people we are dealing with, it is really not surprising that there is so much emotional instability. Not much needs to happen to push someone to the height of his or her aggression, or plunge into the depths of grief. It is easy to grasp some kind of medicine, but that does not offer a real solution. There is a continu-

ous disturbance of balance within us, for which there seems to be no cure. When on top of this all kinds of fake securities are failing, many of us are looking at a hopeless depression.

Still, there is a simple detail that we often lose track of. With many people there is no more flexibility, just because of this lack of balance between healthy tension and relaxation—just in everyday life. We can always point at all kinds of causes outside ourselves, but still it is a fact that when we are making an effort to balance tension, action, work, and concentration with relaxation, letting go, being idle, and directing our attention inward, we will create a firm emotional basis, causing us to stand much firmer in our shoes.

Sounds, especially from our own voice, can be of help here. Sounds can let many pent-up wrath and emotions come out, but they can also be very healing and soothing when there are emotional wounds, like divorce, separation, farewell to loved ones, or juvenile traumas.

One example of this is the singing of vowels and sounds, which can initiate healing, soothing, and discharging the emotions.
You will first need to practice the technique well, before bringing it into practice. Singing with vowels is called *toning*. In chapter 18, this practice will be further described, but below you will see with every vowel a number of qualities that have been experimentally determined. Still, it would be good to realize that these are general patterns, which might not work exactly the same with everybody. They are general tendencies that we can use when dealing with emotions.

Working with sounds can work little miracles with emotional blockades. The list below shows the effects of the various vowels and sound combinations. It appears that the pitch is of less importance here, although you may couple for instance the AH vowel to the pitch of the heart area, the tone F.

UH (as in *true*)	Grounding; feeling more solid in your body; calming, relaxing; feeling of security
OH (as in *coach*)	Awareness; better self-image and identity, individuality; stomach
AH (as in *maharishi*)	Reaching out to the world, feelings from the heart; feeling like creating space
EY (as in *may*)	Being able to express yourself, also listening to the other; communication
EE (as in *see*)	Energy, waking up from lethargy; mental and physical endurance
MM	More balance and harmony; more room in the head; very relaxing
HRAIIIM (*hrahiiimm*)	Expression and neutralizing of sorrow and suffering
EEM-NN-EH	Head, throat, neck and shoulders relax; being able to express yourself
AH-MMAH	Opens the heart, provides room for expression of feelings
OH-MMAEEEH	Centering, connecting head and feet; facilitates expression
HUUMUUMM	Creates a deep grounding and solidity, together with inner tranquility; can also be used when there is fear

You can sing the sound UAIMMM to direct the energy flow in an upward direction, while the sound MIAUUUUU will bring the energy from your head into the body. The latter is important for people who are living too much in their heads (worriers as well as dreamers).

We can add to this list a number of major thirds (threesome sounds) which will emotionally evoke optimistic feelings. All major thirds will have this effect, but as for liberating emotions, therapists like to work with A major.[17]

13 Synchronization and Inner Massage

Sound creates and sound arranges.

There is a third aspect that is just as important for understanding the effects of singing bowls and why they are increasingly being used therapeutically.

This aspect relates to the tendency of objects that make almost identical movements, to move completely synchronistically. Christian Huygens, the 17th-century Dutch scientist, noticed that when two pendulums were placed next to each other, they eventually started to swing in the same tempo. Similarly, after a while, two wave movements that are almost but not quite the same, change and become increasingly similar until they are exactly the same. This is called "the collective arrangement of phases" or synchronization. Women are familiar with this phenomenon in their menstrual cycle. Friends or sisters who live in the same house often menstruate at the same time.

Many people feel that their spirit has been touched when they listen to the living sound of singing bowls. This feeling is less strong when the sound is recorded. Sometimes the sound instills a feeling of great space or profound peace. These and other experiences are not a matter of imagination or belief, as people who have not experienced this phenomenon tend to suggest.

Furthermore, the sense of physical well being after a singing bowl "bath" is not only the result of relaxation.

We have already seen that water is an ideal carrier of vibrations. When you strike a singing bowl you can feel that the air surrounding the bowl also vibrates. People who have never heard of singing bowls and do not know what frequencies are, also experience this when they place their hand against a singing bowl for the first time.

The powerful vibrations spread quickly through our body, which consists of more than 80 percent water after all, resulting in a very delicate internal massage of all the cells. Physiotherapists also make use of this internal massage with ultra-sonic sound waves.

What is meant by the "unification of phases"? The human body is a living entity of vibrations and wavelengths. A healthy organ is well tuned, meaning that it vibrates only at its own frequency, while the frequency of a sick organ is disturbed.

Singing bowls (as well as gongs and tingshaws) recreate the original harmonic frequency, and stimulate the body to rediscover its own harmonic frequency, by making it vibrate to the frequency of the bowl so that when it is synchronized, it can vibrate independently. Stimulated and taken up by the powerful vibrations of the singing bowl, the body is able to tune into its own undisturbed frequency.

14 Shamanism and Brain Waves

In the shamanistic tradition, sound is seen as one way of entering into other worlds and realities. In the past, the access to this other reality was an extremely well-kept secret and could only be achieved after a long period of study, meditation, and special ceremonies. Well into this century, all the teachings and information about what yogis and shamans did in these "trance states" were generally considered as inexplicable "secrets" or even "miracles" or otherwise as clever tricks based on skillful suggestion and sometimes the superstition and credulity of the onlookers.

In the past 10 or 20 years, things have changed. The search for an inner self or inner path has led more and more people to look beyond the teachings of the Christian church. The flood of dogma and liturgical discussion has obscured the guideposts left by Jesus Christ. The path of materialistic thinking seems to be heading toward a literal dead end with the chemical death of the environment.

Christian prayer has been replaced by Eastern meditation techniques and mantras have taken the place of the rosary. Sometimes it is necessary to adopt a new approach to remember and recognize the oldest principles. According to Joska Soos, the second and third shamanistic axioms are: "The secret of all knowledge and the knowledge of all secrets lie in ourselves."

In virtually every religion, sound is used to take the spirit into another realm, where there is a greater receptivity for what is actually nameless and has therefore been given many different names: insight, light, God, the Self.

The Sufi master Hazrat Inayat Khan, who was a famous musician before dedicating himself to his task as a spiritual leader, said that music not only gives people strength but can also transport them to ecstasy. He said that mystics throughout the ages have always loved music above everything else. Sufis have always considered music to be the source of inspiration for their meditations and believe that meditation with music is more fruitful than meditation without it.

The measurement of electromagnetic brain waves has demonstrated that there are a number of clearly recognizable wavelengths, each connected with a different state of consciousness.

When for the first time an appliance was used in the hospital that could actually measure the brain activity—the electroencephalogram (EEG)—it was not only possible to visualize which parts of the brain are active and which are not, but it was also possible to record which combinations of brain waves—very weak electromagnetic currencies—are being produced by the brain: always a mixture of *beta* (more than 14 hertz), *alpha* (9 – 13 Hz), *theta* (4 – 8 Hz) and/or *delta* (0.5 – 3Hz). Generally speaking, the higher the vibratory rate, the more active the brain will be.

An example of the sound affecting consciousness (read: brain waves) we can witness at a building site where piles are being driven into the soft ground, with a rhythm of about one ram per second, matching the wavelength of our brain waves in deep delta. No wonder that those chaps who are always hanging around these sites often seem to be in a kind of trance: that is because of this steady rhythm! Someone in a trance will show brain wave patterns with mainly delta. Likewise, the music at dance parties visited by crowds of youngsters often has the same rhythm—a rhythm they are being exposed to for hours and hours, and moreover with a sound volume nobody (no body) can stand.

Beta – 14 Hz and higher:	are found in our normal waking state of consciousness, when we are active
Alpha – 9 to 13 Hz:	occur in a waking state, calm and relaxed, when we daydream or meditate, feeling good
Theta – 4 to 8 Hz:	occur in states of meditation, clear state of mind, shamanic activities, deeply relaxed
Delta – 0.5 to 3 Hz:	occur in deep sleep, have been found in very profound states of meditation, healing and trance

Of course there is never just one single kind of brain wave in someone's head; brain activity will always be a mixture of various wavelengths, dependant on the state of mind you are in. But what shows is that, for instance, when someone is in deep meditation, there is a balance in activity between both hemispheres, and there are *mainly* alpha and theta brainwaves being produced. Meaning, an area somewhere in between 3 and 10 hertz. In a very deep meditation this may turn out even lower, in the Delta range.

Now suppose someone strikes a singing bowl with a rhythm of one hit per second; provided this continues awhile, we will see the same effect as at the building site: listeners are entering a kind of trance state. Only now in this case it is not a loud ram that might damage our eardrums, but the pleasant, velvet, healing sound of the singing bowl, rich in healing overtones, creating a state of consciousness that can be very relaxing, and healing.

These bowls, in particular, instill a sense of deep relaxation and inner space opening up.

Information in the brain is transmitted through neurons. nerve cells with long, branching offshoots that transmit impulses. This transmission uses the electrochemical properties of the cells to transmit rapid communication waves. Each of the ten billion neurons in the human brain has the potential for 100,000,000 connections. In fact the human brain has unlimited potential. It could be that the freely moving vibration produced by the singing bowls stimulates the neurons to make more connections. If that is the case, this could mean that consciousness is literally being increased.

15 Male and Female

The shape of singing bowls is in many cultures and religions a feminine symbol, while the hammer or rubbing stick is a typical masculine symbol. The metal of the singing bowl originates from the womb of Mother Earth, also a feminine principle. By striking a singing bowl, the air around it will be vibrated, and this vibration continues inside our body, mainly in the body fluids. The element air stands for the masculine principle, while the element water is typically feminine. This way there is a constant exchange between masculine and feminine elements, like we continuously can observe in nature and the whole cosmos. Masculine and feminine supplement each other, they are connected and eventually are one. The sound of the bowl is a beautiful example of these principles. The *striking* of a singing bowl has a masculine element, the *sounding itself* or the *rubbing the rim* is feminine in nature. The sound of the bowl can be very grounding, or it may also open you up for the heavens above— the material and the spiritual. They are not opposed to each other; they work in unison. Likewise, the deep relaxation as a result of the sounds of the singing bowls can make you feel very vivacious and cheerful afterwards.

With your partner you can do an exercise that literally will work in consonance:

Sit facing each other, with a large singing bowl between you. Now you will simply take turns in striking the bowl for a couple of minutes, with a large felt hammer. Just try and trust your gut feeling, and not think too much of how it *should* be. Allow for silence in between the sounds as well. Put all your feeling, your softness, your love in the sounds you make. When you feel you are ready, hand over the hammer to your partner, who will then do the same performance. The one who listens sits with eyes closed, trying to experience and feel completely how these

sounds affect the body, at the surface and deep within. Always try both to keep in touch with a flowing breath. If you feel like it, try releasing your tensions with long, deep sighs!

In another version of this exercise the listening partner can hum along with the sound. Here also try being the observer of everything that is happening, that is perceptible.

Always close with a period of complete silence, holding each other's hands.

Part 4

PRACTICE—A MANUAL

• • • • • • •

Even someone whose life is rooted in knowledge acts
according to his own nature, because everyone behaves
according to his own character.
What then could men achieve by oppression?

Bhagavad-Gita 111.33

16 The Individual Sound Is Always Unique

After reading the first chapters of this book you might think that you would need a great deal of knowledge to find a good singing bowl. Or you might spend a long time looking for a bowl with exceptional inscriptions because that sort of bowl is likely to produce the best sound.

In practice, people sometimes leave the decision to someone else. They may even say to the person selling the bowls, "Find something for me, preferably a good matching pair."

Of course, it is quite possible to do this. But these people are approaching the problem from the outside. Anyone who works with a bowl, whether he likes it or not, embarks on a journey to the inside, toward his own experience, his own harmony or whatever else you might want to call it.

Therefore the most natural way is for you to look for your own bowl. After all, everyone vibrates with a unique frequency, and therefore they will only find their own bowl by listening to it themselves, not with their heads, but with their hearts—and by feeling. Even people who are hard of hearing can enjoy a singing bowl. After all, the vibration is so tangible that it goes straight inside you, and the sensation is not diminished just because you cannot hear the sound. This is very clear with the sacrificial bowls; even though they are never sounded their wave patterns need to be harmonious so that the gifts for the gods are offered harmoniously.

For that reason it is not necessary to worry about finding a bowl that was obviously made as a singing bowl. Although some bowls do have a delightful sound, it is not really the beauty of the sound that matters. There are bowls that sound dissonant, especially to the Western ear, but which nevertheless have a wonderfully liberating effect and these are bowls usually sought after by sound therapists. Anyone who is looking for his own singing bowl is firstly looking for a bowl that will touch him. He is looking for the bowl that makes him take a deep breath and gives him a warm feeling flowing through his body. He feels carried along by the sound, and this is what attracts him. Feel it for yourself. Do not rely on another's judgment about the bowl.

Every person is a unique sounding board and will make the bowl resonate in a completely different way. That is why one bowl will resonate differently for different people. In addition, every person changes from one moment to the next, both physically and spiritually, and therefore the same bowl will sound different at different times. With some people the higher notes resonate longer; with others the higher notes fade quickly and the lower notes continue for a longer period.

Therefore you should not start by looking out for "beautiful" or "ugly" sounds in the usual sense of the word. Do not look for anything exceptional. The sound of every bowl is unique, whether it comes from a small, unattractive bowl or from a magnificent bowl the size of a modest footbath. The only difference is that if you buy the latter, your "own sound" will cost a lot more. Singing bowls are usually sold by weight. There is no point in quoting any prices here as these depend on the person selling the bowl and their prices are always changing. Pricing bowls by weight means that larger ones will be more expensive.

17 A Matter of Choice

There are also different ways of actually choosing a singing bowl you wish to buy. There are people who know whether or not a bowl appeals to them when they have heard it sound just once. They are able to come to an intuitive decision quite quickly.

Someone who feels less certain but who still wants to decide on the basis of intuition can adopt the following method when choosing a bowl.

First place the bowl on a table with a cloth, towel, or other light material between the bowl and the table. Place one or two fingers in the middle of the base of the bowl to keep it still. Now strike the rim of the bowl with a beater that is not too large, let the sound ring out and listen to the tone and resonance of the bowl.

If the bowl seems to be inviting you to a closer acquaintance, take it into the palm of your hand. Stretch out your arm so that you can easily hold the bowl in the hand in front of the body. Strike the bowl once again and let the sound ring out.

Now strike the bowl once again and bring it slowly closer to you. First, bring it near your stomach, a little below the navel. Strike the bowl again. Most importantly, do not listen to the sound with your ears but direct all your attention to your own body. What do you feel? What signals does the body produce as a reflection of the bowl's vibrations?

Take your time. If there is a negative reaction, no matter how slight, this is not a suitable bowl for you at the moment. This is not a judgment regarding the quality of the bowl or about your own personal situation. It merely means that you are not in harmony with this bowl.

If there is no rejection, strike the bowl again and move it upward slowly towards your heart. Then stop, strike the bowl again and leave it to resonate. Again, check your body's reaction.

If there is no negative reaction repeat the process by holding the resonating bowl under your slightly jutting forward chin and then move it up to the base of the nose.

If you take the trouble to get to know a bowl in this way you have a good chance of finding one that is in harmony with you and your body.

If your body seems to reject the bowl strongly and perhaps even results in feelings of nausea, it might be better to forget the idea of working with singing bowls altogether. This does not imply anything good or bad or any other dualistic judgments. It only indicates that there are differences in people and the ways they walk.

Before you leave the house to go looking for your own singing bowl(s), sit down and make a list of the following points, enabling you to be on the alert for every aspect of your quest!

- First of all, take your time! Choosing a singing bowl that suits you well is not something you will do in between running errands and your work. You are not going to use it as a flowerpot; you want to make use of it because of its special, healing qualities. Of course, the rather high prices of good quality singing bowls play a part as well.
- Selecting a personal jewel from a large collection of bowls is almost impossible in a shop filled with clients. So always choose a moment of quietude in the shop, or ask for a specific time after closing hours, or a separate room where you can experiment at ease and without disturbance.
- The acoustics of a room determines partly how a sound is conceived. There are also other (large) objects and furniture that influence the sound. So a singing bowl can sound different in a shop than it does at home.
- Try and use various hammers and rubbing sticks to examine the sounds; a good vendor will have these in stock. If you already have some experience, you can bring your own of course.
- Look to see if the singing bowl you examine is undamaged and whole: is it completely round, does it have any dents or other blemishes?
- Listen to the basic tone and the harmonic overtones. How many overtones can you hear (mainly during the rubbing

around the rim)? You should be able to distinguish at least three or four tones—that is, if you value this of course If you are completely enchanted by a bowl without an overtone richness, that is fine also. If need be, take along another instrument like a xylophone or a flute, to check the purity of the tones.

- Check if the sound continues for a long time after striking the bowl. The sound of a good singing bowl with the right alloy will last a long time. Also, distinguish between the basic tone and the overtones.
- Make sure the bowl can be rubbed evenly around the rim. With some bowls this is hardly possible, and that is a pity because then you will miss an essential part of the possibilities.
- Most important is that you always feel good with what the sound will do to you. What do *you* feel? What goes through *your* mind (and body) when you hear and feel the sound? You need to open yourself completely to all these sensations, of course, otherwise nothing will happen. Never let yourself be talked into something you do not want. The sound should appeal to you one hundred percent, otherwise the deal is off!
- It may also be advisable—certainly when it is your first time—to go shopping in different stores, before making your final choice.

If at any time you wish to buy a second or third singing bowl or even more, take the bowl or bowls that you already have with you, unless you have too many. But by that time you will know how to choose a bowl anyway. It is not necessary to have a series of bowls of greatly differing sizes. And it is impossible to assemble a "singing bowl orchestra" with the melodious harmonies we know in the West.

The clear, floating sound of the singing bowl produces harmonies that are quite different from those that we are used to. By striking two or three bowls immediately after each other you can discover completely new harmonies and chords, and you will have a physical sense of whether or not they will appeal to you.

If you have finally found your own singing bowl—or bowls—of course you will want to find a nice spot for it at home—out of reach of children and pets, in a place of honor; a place where such splendid works of art are shown to full advantage, possibly together with a beautiful houseplant, other works of art, or large crystals;.a nice ensemble, beautiful to look at!

If you are so privileged to have in your home a separate room or special corner you can retreat in silence, of course that will be an ideal place to keep your singing bowl(s).

18 Overtone Singing

A singing bowl can be used before meditating, for becoming still, but also together with singing and experiencing of overtones, a special way of using your own singing voice.

There is a technique that may cause a very special perception of sound. With this technique, the overtones of the bowl are resonated by way of your oral cavity. First do some preliminary exercises, using your voice to make beautiful harmonic overtones. While singing a single tone (pitch) you can hear the overtones by singing successive vowels in this particular pitch and shaping your lips, oral cavity, and tongue well, according to each and every vowel. So singing while your breath lasts from AH to OH, or from EY to OH, or just by singing words like MOOOY or AOUM, you can produce very beautiful, audible overtones; first softly, and gradually, with a little practice, more clearly.

Now the special technique goes like this: Hold the bowl on top of your fingertips, or in the palm of your hand, and keep it parallel to your face, about 10 to 15 inches away from your mouth. By moving the rim of the singing bowl (after striking it with a hammer) closer to your lips, and shaping your mouth—without making a sound yourself—as if you were singing overtones, you can often "pick up" the whole range of overtones from the bowl and hear these inside and outside your body. This way you become as one with the bowl and the beautiful sounds. Move the bowl a little back and forth to "catch" the best sound. The ideal distance between the edge of the bowl and your mouth should be approximately just a quarter of an inch to two inches. Just try and find out for yourself!

Then, repeat this same process while using your own voice, of course at the same pitch as the singing bowl. This technique not only reveals other sound aspects of the bowl, but also has a more inwardly directing effect. The sound vibrations resonate directly in the body's cavities, mainly those of the head, throat, and chest. This way, your experience of the sound inside your body will be amplified. Small singing bowls work the best this way with the sound of OU. Experiment also with various series of sounds, like: *owah-owah-uwah* or *eeah-eeah-eeaaah.*

You need to master the technique of overtone singing before you will be able to combine this with the sounds of your singing bowl. The overtones are (partly) created by flattening or rounding of your tongue. Once you have mastered the technique of overtone singing a little more, you could try singing along with the tone of the singing bowl and then create your own ranges of voice overtones. By doing this while keeping your mouth just above the bowl's edge, you may experience that one of those overtones will suddenly start to resonate in the bowl, and conversely the sound of the bowl will resonate directly inside your body. This is an awesome experience that goes far beyond any description. To say there does not seem to be any boundaries anymore between body and singing bowl, and that everything *becomes* sound, would be just an indistinct attempt.

Another way to transfer the harmonic overtones of a singing bowl directly into your body is really is a very special experience. You do need a rather large singing bowl, which you then hold very close in front of your chest, or head. Start by hitting the bowl softly, and experiment how loud you can make the sounds. Some people can handle just a soft volume; others may stand a pretty loud sound. The next step will then be to concentrate on the overtones of the bowl, which will directly enter your head and body, and you may also try singing along with the sounds, using various vowels. Here also, the pauses of silence in between the sounds are an essential part of your experience.

19 Water

In chapter 6 we mentioned a special kind of singing bowl filled with water, resonating in specific patterns. But we can also experiment with other regular, large singing bowls and water.

A simple way is to fill the singing bowl with just a shallow bit of water. Begin with a small amount and gradually add more. Some bowls even have ring markings around the inside to indicate where the water level should be for a certain kind of effect. But the only way to find out for yourself is to experiment and discover what sounds best. So, by continually adding water to the bowl you can see what effect the water has on the sound, but also what the sound does to the water. For the first effect, you can also wiggle and rotate the bowl, so the water will begin rotating, and use the felt hammer and the rubbing stick. Regarding

the second effect, you can see which patterns are being created in the water by the sound. Perhaps you may even own a fountain bowl, a star bowl (see picture on page 85). Sometimes a singing bowl will sound much faster with a beautiful, long-lasting tone when it is filled with water, up to a certain level.

Another very special experience is creating *glissandi*, gliding sounds that are best compared to a wailing cat, but much nicer! For this you need to fill the singing bowl with just a little bit of water and then strike or rub it (striking works better in this experiment). By wiggling the bowl carefully, the back and forth lapping water will cause slight differences in the sound: the glissandi. With a little more experience and skill, you might even be able to do this with a bowl in each hand, causing an interaction between both tones and overtones. This will become a magical mystery tour when performing this together with four or five others!

Another special variant is hanging a small singing bowl halfway in the water inside a large bowl. Keep the small bowl between your finger tips and hang it with just its bottom in the water, then strike the large bowl firmly with a felt hammer. You will then hear the small bowl resonate in the higher realms of the overtones from the large one. It will work best when both singing bowls have been tuned in the same key.

20 Sound Sets

As described above, you can get to know a multitude of different aspects of a singing bowl. If you have several bowls there are obviously more discoveries to be made. I would just like to mention a few more here.

The most important discovery is what the bowls sound like together. What sound do they make when they are struck (or ribbed) at the same time? Can you tell the sounds apart, do they contrast with each other, do they harmonize? Do they cancel each other out (same wavelengths) or do they combine well to create new sounds (connection of phases)?

By listening carefully, it is possible to get some idea of the wave forms that are created when two sounds meet. Some bowls seem to produce the same sound at first, but still you can immediately feel they are different. The difference can be discov-

ered by listening intently. The difference may be in the audible oscillations or in the harmonics, which may differ.

The interaction of two singing bowls played together varies from one pair to another. An example would be two bowls of about the same size, which struck simultaneously produce such strong harmonics that all kinds of "phantom" tunes may be created in between them, these can also be sung by creating the harmonics using the mouth held precisely in between the two bowls held closely together.

I witnessed a truly remarkable pattern of coordinated vibration with two singing bowls, when the larger of the two was placed upside down and the smaller was placed the right way up on top of the larger one. When the smaller bowl was gently rotated with a rubbing stick it then started rotating—literally!— of its own accord, and the two bowls together made a strange, whistling, gliding tone.

A singing bowls therapist will use multiple bowls, placing them on and around the body of the person who will receive treatment. Then they are being struck or rubbed, one by one or sometimes together at the same time. There are also special chakra sets that are placed on, or held above the areas of these energy centers. In the picture you will also see singing bowls near the feet and head.

You can also use the sound massage on yourself. When you have more than one singing bowl at your disposal, you can place these in front of you while you are sitting on the floor, on a pillow, or meditation bench. You can then strike them one by one, or you pick one up and rub it. Allow the sounds always to ring to the very last vibration. You can also strike two or more attuned bowls at the same time or shortly after each other. When you know there is some kind of energy block and/or pain in your body, you could hold a large bowl just in front of this area and strike or rub it, for a few minutes, while breathing deeply, sighing out. Follow your gut feeling; your body will tell you when it is enough. Sometimes you need to be silent for a while, and then continue with the sounds once more.

21 Sounding: Methods and Tools

Singing bowls produce their singing tones in different ways. The first thing you will need is a gong beater. The size of this beater depends on the bowl being struck. There are no real guidelines for this.

Gong beaters, especially those covered with felt or fleece, are beaters for percussion instruments. Picking the perfect beater is a matter of trial and error, as every bowl has its own special requirements. One bowl will sound better with a softer beater, while others need a harder beater.

As a rule, a larger gong beater will produce the full richness of sound in a large bowl, while it is better to use smaller beaters for the smaller bowls. In fact, many different beaters can be used on any bowl. Every beater produces a different sound from the range of the basic note and its harmonics. Apart from the recognized gong beaters covered with felt, fleece, cork, rope, or wood, you can use your own hands as percussion instruments: the heel of your hand, your fingers, or nails.

If you enjoy experimenting, you can try using almost anything as a beater. You can use just one beater or try working with two of the same shape. If you give full rein to your ingenuity and your love for playing the singing bowls, you will discover many surprising things.

Striking a singing bowl with a beater needs to be very different from striking a gong. This requires a lot of practice and technique to do it right. The most important part is that you do not try to bang into it as hard as you can. It should be done in a much more subtle way. Even though you move the beater fairly fast toward the bowl's rim, just when it hits the rim you pull back. So it is just a light bop rather than a heavy blow.

It is obvious that a felt hammer will produce a completely different sound than a wooden beater. That is why a wooden beater is not often used, for instance when activating the energy

of a chakra. But when you use a wooden beater without wrapping it will produce a clear, clean sound with at least two or three overtones. So more often singing bowls are being struck by beaters with balls made of felt, flannel, or even fur, or ones wrapped with rope, leather, suede, felt, or rubber, even adhesive plastic or plaster. The wooden beaters are made of hardwood (oak, for instance) or softwood (such as balsa or birch). And of course, every material has its own characteristic sound. So because of this wide variety of beaters and hammers you can elicit a multitude of sounds from one singing bowl.

Rubbing or *rotating* is another technique we use to set the tones of a bowl ringing. This is a rotating movement with a smooth stick around the outside rim. This produces an effect similar to rubbing a wet finger along the rim of a crystal glass. A full singing tone is heard and will steadily increase in volume, and may be so intense that the glass will break. This accounts for the term "singing bowls." According to some authorities, the former shamans of the Himalayas also used the singing bowls like this to produce the singing sound. It is best to rub with a round stick or club made of hardwood, which you hold against the rim of the bowl at about 45 degrees while rotating the stick around the rim. This creates the sound of one basic tone, with on top of that—mostly less audible—the harmonic overtones. These are very easy to discern with singing bowls, and we can hear by the purity of these overtones if it is a good singing bowl: it should be perfectly round, have a perfectly spherical shape—a u-shape or more like a dish—and regularly beaten, cast, or turned (on a lathe) from one piece of metal.[18] In most cases, especially with old singing bowls, you need first to strike the bowl with the stick once, so as to *create* a good initial vibration, then *continue* the tone by rotating the stick along the rim. Singing bowls that are cast or turned, as well as bowls with thick metal, are generally easily rubbed, with a nice, full tone.

Another way of rubbing, causing the overtones—and even undertones—to be heard very well, is by rotating the stick almost vertically around the outer rim. This may even cause the overtones to drown out the basic tone! Of course it takes practice to produce these effects.

Intensifying the overtones relates to the angle of the rubbing stick with respect to the rim of the bowl, but also to the bowl itself—the shape and the metal compound—and finally to the velocity of rotating the stick.

The angle of the stick against the rim determines the complexity of overtones: slanted at 60 to 45 degrees to a vertical rim, it will produce more high tones, while held almost vertically, it creates much deeper tones.

The rotating often begins with a rather swift movement, but once the tone is fully audible you can rotate the stick slower, to eventually maintain this tone at full strength. By varying the velocity in a certain rhythm you will get a change in volume as well, which results in a very special effect. This effect may be applied specifically: a rhythm of one change per second works very well and is even soporific (read the section about brain wave patterns in chapter 14).

Instead of rubbing with a stick, some players use a fiddle-stick; this requires even more skill and there are but a few players who master this technique.

The thinner the stick used to strike a bowl, the higher the tone that is produced. Thus it is best to use a fairly thin stick on smaller bowls with a high tone.

It is extremely difficult, however, to work on really large bowls with a thin stick. The vibration of the rim of a large bowl can be so great that the stick begins to "dance," causing an unpleasant rattling sound.

You can prevent this rattling in several ways. You can press firmly and evenly against the rim of the bowl while you are turning it to prevent the stick from rattling. It is also possible to use a thicker stick. The pestle of a large wooden mortar could be very suitable. Finally, there is another technique that does not involve rubbing the stick around the rim of the bowl, but consists

of rubbing it backwards and forwards in one particular place on the rim. It is often easier to use this method to produce a singing tone with a really large singing bowl.

With all these methods, the pressure and the speed at which the bowl is rubbed have an influence on the sound and the pitch of the tone produced.

The penetrating singing sound that is created by rubbing the bowl is due to the fact that in this way one of the harmonics is accentuated and developed. To avoid the sound of wood on metal from becoming unpleasant, many owners of singing bowls put tape on their sticks on the part that touches the bowl. This tape should be strong and smooth to avoid any abrasive sound and to prevent the tape being worn away by the rubbing. Stretchable plastic wrap, such as the transparent sort used to cover books, also works very well.

This summary shows that really anything is possible. Many people make their own sticks for their bowls. I have seen sticks made of flannel wrapped around hard rope, sticks made of a long strip of felt boiled in starch and then wrapped tightly around the stick. Other rubbing sticks were covered with the inner tube of a bicycle or made from a wooden pan handle. Personally, I sometimes use the fork of a teak wood salad server set that, if it is used carefully, produces a marvelous, clear high tone with some of my bowls.

Support

For a full, unobstructed sound, the singing bowl needs to have as little contact as possible with the surface that it rests on. You can put the bowl on a soft rug, on a pretty pillow, or just on a stack of the rubber rings of canning jars. If you want to play just one bowl—for not too long, and depending on the size of course—you may also place it in the palm of your hand, or better still, on your fingertips. It is a very special experience when you strike a large singing bowl resting on your flat  palm. Its vibrations will resonate through your arm and your whole body—a wonder-full experience!

There are also beautifully decorated textile rings available in various diameters to use as a solid and good-looking base for your bowls. Another decorative and versatile aid is a hand-carved wooden tripod, suitable for almost every size of singing bowls. Crystal singing bowls usually come with a thick white rubber ring, supporting these vulnerable works of art very solidly.

Of course which support you should use also depends on the shape of the bowl. A bowl with a rather round bottom will not stand on a flat surface, so you need a ring or tripod. But the same applies to a very large bowl with a very flat bottom; if you put such a bowl on a rug, a lot of the sound would be lost. So here again you have to discover which support suits the singing bowl best, in order to produce the optimum sound.

Summary

Singing bowls are mostly played in two ways, with two basic techniques: striking (beating) and rubbing (rotating). The bowls are stricken by means of (mostly felt) hammers of various sizes, and sometimes also fiercely with the fiddlestick. By striking you will hear the gong effect, from subtly light with the small bowls to impressively loud and literally perceptible in the whole body, or certain parts of the body.

The rubbing happens mainly with a handy piece of spar, which may also be wrapped with textile, suede, or rubber bands. By rubbing, a constant basic tone will be audible, with accents in volume, caused of course by varying the velocity of rotating the stick, or applying a firmer or lesser pressure against the rim of the bowl.

22 Guidance in Wonderland

Anyone who owns his own singing bowl has access to a magic land of great variety. There is so much to discover, to experiment with, to hear and to experience in the bowl and your inner self. The way inward is open to you.

For more than a year I had only one bowl and it gave me great pleasure. It was all I needed. I constantly discovered new things and I had to assimilate what I had discovered. I still do not know all the possibilities this bowl offers.

Nevertheless, it is possible to put up some signposts in this magic land that will show the way along paths to be followed, even though every path is a strictly personal experience. These are some of the ways to work with singing bowls and to explore their possibilities step by step.

Listening

Listening to a singing bowl begins quite simply by sitting in a relaxed manner. Then, hold the bowl in the palm of your hand, or put it on a firm cushion, a rubber ring (e.g., of a preserving jar) or on a soft cloth in front of you. Let the sound ring out. Listen to it with closed eyes. Start by experiencing the sound as a whole. Once you are familiar with the sound of the bowl, you can begin to listen to it analytically.

To distinguish the pitch of the various notes and to get to know and understand the nature of every tone, it is worth remembering that sound has a form and a wavelength. As you listen, try to distinguish the pulse of the various tones. Is the subharmonic tone vibrating faster or slower than the dominant basic note? Do they harmonize easily with each other, for example by one being exactly two or three times faster than the other, or is the difference more difficult to measure: e.g., in a set amount of time, does one make five oscillations to the other's three?

Traditional Tibetan singing bowl with decoration of trails.

A set of singing bowls in several sizes and formats. Only the three smallest bowls were produced recently.

Striking a big Bengalese singing bowl with a felt hammer – an impressive sound!

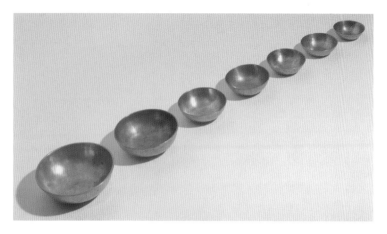

Above: a set of seven singing bowls, attuned to the seven chakras, the body's energy centers.

Below: a classic Tibetan singing bowl with wooden beater.

By striking a big, water filled singing bowl, the water is set into vibration in a spectacular way. This can only happen when the bowl is rubbed instead of struck.

The singing bowl sounds through the vibrations of the voice. Interaction between bowl and voice.

The stick is rubbed gently but firmly against the rim of the singing bowl in order to produce a pure basic tone with harmonic overtones.

Below: a diversity of singing bowls in a wholesaler's warehouse.

Illustrations of ting-shaws, bells and dorje. The buddha statue holds a dorje vertically in front of the heart.

By concentrating on one tone and, if necessary, following it with movements of the hand or body, it is possible to perceive not only different tones, but also different wave patterns in one bowl.

However, sounds are much more than a wave pattern of straight lines; they also have a three dimensional shape. There are examples such as the expanding ripples caused by a stone thrown into still water, or the inner spirals of a whirlpool. You can discover these different sound forms by listening with your whole body, not just your ears.

You can also hold the bowl at different distances from your body, or even place it on different parts of your body, and listen again to see if you can hear a difference.

When you have tried all this, it is a good idea to stop analyzing and allow the sound of the bowl to exist as a whole. Even when the sound has apparently died away completely you can still listen with your inner ear. Where has the sound gone? What do you hear in the ensuing silence? What is the sound of your own body? Of your essence? Of the silence?

Feeling

There are different ways of feeling the sound. If you place a singing bowl near or actually on your body you can feel the vibrations going through your body. One bowl may have a wave pattern consisting of large waves, another may have a sound that produces smaller, localized vibrations, and yet another can give the impression of the sound going straight through your body. By lying down in a relaxed way and placing the bowl on different parts of your body, such as the stomach or chest, or even the head, you can observe the effects of the sound in as many ways as possible. Sitting in a chair you can try putting the bowl on your feet or thighs and knees. In this way you can feel the different physical sensations as well as the different sounds. With larger bowls particularly, it is possible to feel the vibrations of the bowl when you hold your hand at some distance from the edge, where they are felt as a flow of warm air radiating from the bowl. When you are able to feel these vibrations you can try and sense the whole sound shapes around and inside the bowl. An-

other way of feeling the sound vibrations and absorbing them into your body is to stroke the side of the bowl immediately after it has been struck.

It is also possible to touch the vibrating bowl with your tongue or lips. With closed eyes, and without touching the bowl with any part of the body, you can try to feel where the sound is vibrating most strongly, and what feelings are evoked in different parts of the body—feelings of release, relaxation, order, or stimulation.

After these exercises and this concentration on the body's reception to the sound, it may also be helpful to return to the pure sound itself and to allow it to continue to sing without thinking or trying to analyze it in any way. Do exactly what the bowl does: set the air in motion. Breathe out strongly. Take a few deep, relaxed breaths. Experience and insight come to us particularly when we are able to let go.

Observing
You can clearly see the vibrations on the edge of a bowl that has just been struck. By observing this movement you will see different vibrations at the same time, and in this way discover something about the shape of the sound. With these exercises you can tune into the sound better, and you will be able to per-

ceive the pattern of vibrations beyond the audible spectrum, even after the sound has ended. The sound of the bowl can be internalized to such an extent that it becomes possible to perceive the vibrations of the bowl just by looking at it and without even touching it.

Anyone who becomes so intensely involved with sound could, after a time, develop an inner experience of the relationship between form and sound and even see visions of geometric shapes: the shape of the sound imprints itself directly on the inner retina, without the intervention of a medium such as water, or sand on a sheet of glass.

Harmonics

A very special sensation can be achieved by using a technique in which the harmonics of the bowl resonate more strongly with the help of the oral cavity. When you sing a single note you can produce the harmonics by singing successive vowels with the same note and in this way moving your mouth cavity and tongue into the shape of each vowel.

By singing from A to o or from E to o in one breath, or just by singing a word such as "boy" in one breath, you can produce the harmonics, at first softly and gradually, with more practice, more clearly.

By placing the mouth near the rim of the singing bowl and allowing the mouth to form the vowels in the way described above, you can often separate out the different harmonics. To do this, hold the bowl at precisely 90 degrees to the place where you struck the rim. Again, it is a matter of trial and error. This technique not only makes another aspect of the bowl's sound audible, it also has an internal effect. The vibrations reverberate in the body cavities, especially those in the head, throat, and chest and this allows the sound to be experienced in yet another physical way.

Anyone who has learned to sing with harmonics, with a great deal of practice, can also try to sing a tone from the bowl aloud and then the harmonics above it. By doing this just above the edge of the bowl you will find that one of these harmonics will suddenly start to resonate in the bowl itself, and the sound of the bowl then directly reverberates in your body. It is almost impossible to describe this experience in which body and sound seem to melt into one vibrating unity.

Water

A simple way to make discoveries with a bowl is to fill it with water. Begin with a small amount and gradually add more. If there are any rings around the inside of the bowl these could indicate how full the bowl must be to produce the desired effect. But again, discoveries are made only by experimenting.

By continually adding water to the bowl you can see what effect the water has on the sound produced, and vice versa. First, rotate the bowl so that the water itself is rotating, and strike and rub the rim. Secondly, look at the patterns in the water in the bowl. It may actually be a fountain bowl.

Sometimes a bowl produces a beautiful, penetrating singing tone more rapidly by being rubbed if it is filled with water to a certain level.

23 An Open Heart, an Open Mind

It is worth repeating that singing bowls can give access to a field of unlimited possibilities, both by experimenting with them and through their internal effects. That is not to say that it is necessary or even desirable to travel through this field in as many directions as possible. Firstly, the singing bowl is something we should enjoy, without any ulterior motives. Preconceived ideas of possible experiences will only be an obstacle to what is actually happening. If you are impatient to discover something, it can take a lot longer.

This means that anyone who expects something from sound will make the greatest discoveries by not expecting anything. An open heart and an open mind are, in the end, the most reliable signposts on the path leading inwards—both into sound and into yourself. When you hear something or experience something, in any form, it is important to take note of the experience, feel it and then let it go. Do not attach any great significance to it. Do not draw any particular conclusions. Remember that everyone undergoes changes and therefore influences sound in different ways. Most of the phenomena you have experienced, will recur. If they do not, then at least you will have enjoyed them without being attached to them, leaving the way open for more experiences.

24 Sound Therapeutics

Singing bowls have an unmistakable effect on people. Because of this they are increasingly used as therapeutic aids. We can only guess what the original makers and users of these bowls, whoever they may have been, would think about this. Although our holistic way of thinking makes no distinction between the body and the spirit, we still find it difficult not to make a distinction and to ignore the analytical thought processes we are so accustomed to using. On the other hand, the shamanistic approach of making no distinction, was a very different one. It was an approach that was not based on intellectual or rediscovered ideas, but was unformed and unspoiled. It was a natural approach that was simply experienced. We cannot think in these ways nowadays; we should not aim to do as they did. All we can do is to follow our own path, at the same time learning from the old traditions.

Anyone who feels the urge and intention to work with singing bowls for the benefit of others (as sound therapists or in combination with other techniques)—following their own personal voyage of discovery into sound and its effects on the body and the soul—can find out about the different ways of working from practicing sound therapists and by being treated by them. Anyone who is interested in sound but does not necessarily want their own singing bowl may find that a treatment with sound or a concert or demonstration is a good introduction to the workings of sound.

Sound therapists also sometimes do workshops in which the perception of sound and the ways in which sound works are examined in greater depth. At these sessions, like-minded people meet and can work together on the path of learning. They can make arrangements to use each other as subjects after the workshop to discover and try out ever more things together.

Later on, those who feel confident enough can gradually start to apply what they have learned to their own family and friends. For the learning process it is important to choose volunteers who are prepared to tell you what they are experiencing at every stage. In this way the prospective therapist can assess what is happening and what effects have been evoked. At a later stage, when "official" patients are being treated, it is not always possible to ask what is happening and what has been experienced. Many people cannot describe their experiences or prefer to assimilate them in silence. That is why exploration and practice are just as important in sound therapy as in any other therapeutic technique.

So carefulness is required. As with other therapies, you need to know what you are doing before you start. Do not even think of playing therapist with a few bowls when you don't have the experience. Although in most cases it will not hurt very badly— that would require many hours of continuous sounds—you need to become the expert before imagining being a singing bowls therapist. First the experience, and then you will need also the intensive coaching of another expert practitioner. And, of course, for a sound therapeutic practice you would need a rather large collection and variety of bowls, and that is something that may take years. Good quality singing bowls are not cheap, and only after many years will you be able to tell which collection

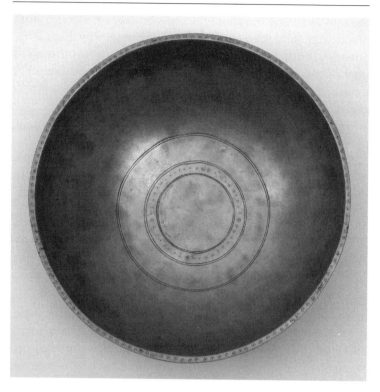

works best for you personally. Finally, there are of course the legal regulations you need to comply with to protect the authentic therapeutic practice.

So, sound advice for a good practice: if you think you have built up enough experience and wish from your heart to use the singing bowls in a therapeutic practice—possibly as part of several other approaches, like working with (semi)precious stones, herbs, massage—then go and look for someone who is competent enough to train you and coach you. If you are truly ready, you will find that person!

25 Crystal Singing Bowls

Crystal singing bowls are something special indeed.[19] For sound clarity and sound volume these bowls are at a solitary altitude, also regarding their usage: we can only utilize these sounds sparingly and selectively. The best comparison I can think of is this: metal singing bowls—the bigger ones, certainly—have a sound that is "straight," down to earth, while crystal singing bowls miss this earth element—their sounds are "etheric" in nature. Energy healers will say that the sounds of the crystal singing bowls mainly work at the energy bodies, while the metal ones also have a direct physical effect. Of course, this distinction is not entirely true, because the vibrations of a crystal bowl will also resonate in our bodies, but apparently the healing effects are mainly energetic.

Crystal singing bowls are actually not made of crystal; they are produced out of rhinestone (quartz, silicon dioxide). The compound is made from quartz, sand, and water, heated up to 7,200° (about 4,000° C); this process is called *quartz fusion*. The liquid material is cast in a mold, and after coagulation the bowls are tuned with modern adjusting equipment up to a hundredth of a tone. This is a professional process that requires the utmost precision, but the results are magical. The bowls are smooth on the inside and slightly rugged and opaque on the outside, and transparent.

Crystal singing bowls are extremely fragile; during play as well as transport you need to be very careful. But in concert they are beautiful eye (and ear) catchers, especially when combined with a show of colored lights shining behind the bowls.

Some people take the view that crystal singing bowls are not right for a sound massage or sound therapy. They claim that the intensive vibrations may strike someone out of balance. This is the comment of Danny Becher, a sound therapist with many

years of experience, on this matter: "If that is the intention of the player, yes, this might happen. But you can do the same with very small singing bowls (either metal or crystal ones), or even with a single word. The insight and experience of the player of the instruments remains of the utmost importance—how his awareness of the energy is, and mainly what his intentions are. The bigger singing bowls are able to produce very intense, dynamic sounds, and fill a big room with their sounds, but we can also work with these in a very subtle way—not with the strongest volume possible, but with the softness of a light breath—the fine sounds working deep, with body, a sound that can be delivered very supportive, tender and enchanting."

It's clear that crystal singing bowls produce a very special sound that is so different from that of metal ones. There are people who just do not like them, find them too aloof, but it happens all the time that the same people, once they get used to the sounds, fall in love with them! So it is important that we listen to these sounds without prejudice. Most singing bowl players use combinations of metal and crystal bowls, with truly magical effects. It often happens after a concert that people tell their stories of all kinds of special perceptions and experiences.

You may also use the sounds of a CD recording as a background during a yoga session or a massage. The continuous sound atmosphere will then accord perfectly with the experience of breath and relaxation.

The crystal singing bowls are also commercially offered in sets of seven chakra tones, with sticks in the colors of the seven chakras, or even the bowls themselves in those colors. The bowls are produced in the United States, but are distributed worldwide.

In Europe there are also glass singing bowls supplied to the trade. These are cut from large glass tubes and fused at the base. They come in various beautiful colors, they are much cheaper, but they definitely do not have the same sound, and do not even come close to the quality of the crystal bowls!

26 Planet Singing Bowls

In chapter 5 we already spoke about the metals that are energetically associated with a certain planet (energy). Some readers will now think we are getting a little hypothetical here, vague nonsense without any accurate support, but this is not quite true. The idea of planet tones was conceived by Swiss scientist Hans Cousto and elaborated into a system that since has been admired by all scientists (explained in his famous works *The Octaves* and *The Cosmic Octave*). The planet's revolution time is "octave jumped" to an audible vibration.[20] You could say that when you sing a tone D (146.84 Hz, resonating in the lower belly area, associated with the second chakra, and, for instance, the sex organs), a child or a soprano would be able to sing just one or two octaves above this tone D. When you "octave jump up," you will eventually end up at the color blue. But when you "octave jump down," after 33 times you will end up at the revolution time of planet Mars.

Therapists have claimed for many years that there is a certain correlation between the position of the stars and our health.

Many books have been written about the subject, and it has nothing to do with mysterious invisible connections between those far-away heavenly bodies and ourselves, but there are certain energy constellations here, on our own Earth, for every moment in time a kind of blueprint is reflected in the position of the stars and planets. Our sojourn here on Earth is partly determined by these constellations.

And now it turns out that we can add here an extra sound dimension, by working with singing bowls with the corresponding "tones of the planets." Of course it is not that these bowls have been made as planet bowls; it was rather the other way around. The therapist would look for singing bowls matching the planet characteristics (pitch, sound, and energy of a certain bowl) with the body organs. Still, a lot of research needs to be done before we can really make this application worthwhile. Of course, in the end it is all about the effects we can create with this new approach. They say that in very ancient cultures the seers used sounds in such ways. Today we may give these ideas a new place in our modern society, make way for the "new thinking," with our hearts!

In crystal singing bowls as well as metal ones, there are now sets available of planet tones. Of course you can compile a set of your own, to your own insight and liking. One singing bowl in D does not sound the same as another! Pitches also have a certain kind of emotional effect, related to the energy levels in the body. For instance, a C-major is calming and harmonizing. The well-known AOUM (or OM) mantra is mostly sung in this pitch, and the temple bells of the Far East sound mostly in C or C-major.[21] An F creates clarity in the head, and F-major can help during meditation and mystical experiences. Dreamers will need a grounding tone like D or G.

It is advisable not to "just for the fun of it" experiment with this. In this matter, the rule is that you ask for the guidance of an experienced therapist. For instance, many people will not be able to cope well with the F tone, because they need to be grounded first with the help of lower tones.

Anyway, go with your feelings: if it feels one hundred percent right, you can go on. If it does not feel good, stop immediately!

Below you see a specification of the planets with their associated tones and colors.

Planet	Tone	Frequency	Color
Sun	B-major/C	126,22 Hz	some say yellow/green, others gold/yellow
Mercury	C-major/D	141,27 Hz	turquoise/blue
Venus	A	221,23 Hz	orange/yellow
Mars	D	144,72 Hz	light blue
Jupiter	F-major	183,58 Hz	purple/red
Saturn	D	147,85 Hz	blue
Uranus	G-major	207,36 Hz	orange/red
Neptune	G-major	211,44 Hz	orange
Pluto	C-major/D	140,25 Hz	blue/green

27 Meditation, Sounds, and Singing Bowls

There are many kinds of meditation. We know the Western kind, meaning a reflection about a chosen subject, mostly in a religious context. Although Eastern kinds of meditation are often also related to Buddhist or Hindu schools, it is also possible to make these meditations very personal, without the rituals from a religion. Vipassana meditation offers such a way, a very simple way to bring your awareness into the now and live it in its entirety, without judging, without criticism, without opinion. With such a meditation you may use an object to concentrate your attention on, for instance a flower, a candle, or a beautiful quartz crystal, but for this purpose you can also use a singing bowl, provided you have already felt and experienced these bowls to be very good and harmonizing for you. By directing your full attention to the sound—the striking, its duration, its intensity, the timbre, the overtones, the clarity, and finally also the silence after the sound—you will be able to put everything around you and your thoughts "on hold" for a while, and literally come to yourself. This in itself can be a meditation. It may also serve as an introduction to a long-term meditation in complete silence.

We know already (read chapter 14) that the sound of the bowls will create a harmonic balance, mentally as well as physically. You can use this fact as a core for your meditation.

When you strike a large singing bowl and hold it close to your face, you can actually feel it resonate inside, to all cavities—eyes, ears, nose, mouth, throat, and the brain, of course. With each stroke of the felt hammer you can concentrate on another part of your skull, to really feel the resonance there. This resonance creates harmonic, harmonizing vibrations inside your whole head, and works also on your mind as a delicious sound cleansing and resting point.

You can also use your own voice along with these sounds. Sing along in several vowels, like I-E-A-O-U, or an ensemble of vowels and consonants, like MEEAAOOAY, AAOOUUMM—endless combinations are possible—and feel what they do. You can also sing or hum along in another pitch, like three tones above the basic tone of the singing bowl, or the pitch of its first overtone. In time you will discover exactly which tones and sound combinations make you feel good, and work for you.

Always experience intensely the silence after the sound, after the singing bowl completely stops vibrating; in that moment it is as if silence feels more silent than before the sound—a very special experience. Most people who experience this can remain much easier "inside," in the harmonious silence inside their heads, witnessing the flow of the breath, nothing else. Just being there, in the here and now.

Some people have a singing bowl present in their workplace, which they use now and then to do a mini-meditation, just for a few minutes: one strike, one harmonious sounding, eyes closed, and being there with just this sound, nothing else. Why not? A delicious short break like that can help you relax and focus again, and then go on with whatever you were doing.

As practiced in singing bowl therapy, with our sound meditation we can also use a combination of color, scent and other elements to enhance and ameliorate our meditations. This, of course, is a very personal choice. One person likes the pleasant scent of incense or scented oils, the other likes a beautiful green lamp or candle. The more you do these meditations, the less you will need these outer details for your meditation practice. Eventually, you will not even need the sounds anymore. Then, silence will be best—that perfect silence within.[22]

Nada Yoga is a kind of yoga practice using sounds; first with the outer sounds of voice and instruments, and later on with the inner sounds of the spiritual realms. Although this kind of yoga is not so well-known in the West, there are schools and communities teaching this yoga of sound. Singing bowls can play an important role in this practice.[23]

28 Children and Singing Bowls

Many children are by nature attracted to the sounds of singing bowls. Of course they need to be taught prudence in handling the bowls by themselves, but you can carefully introduce them to these—in their eyes—magical instruments. Let them literally feel in their own bodies what will happen when a singing bowl is struck. Let them play with the sounds. Most of all, let them experience for themselves what they like best.

Of course, the playful approach is the best with children. Do not make it too serious. I once did the following test: in a circle of seven children (four girls and three boys), I handed out singing bowls of several sizes and sounds, together with a bold felt beater for each bowl. First I gave a few details about the sounds and the effects, and demonstrated some of them. Then, every child was allowed to beat its own bowl and let it ring out completely. First with their eyes open, then another round with their eyes closed. I had them "feel" the silence afterwards as well. What stood out was that no one in the group thought it was "nuts"; they were all very open and involved in what happened. Next, the children would say a word, the first that came up, about "their" bowl. Words came up like *heavy, round, ticklish, vibrating, loudspeaker.* When I asked the children to do another round, and then give their bowl to someone they thought it would suit, I did not allow them to think for a long time about that, otherwise personal favors would interfere with their spontaneous choice. Although it did not work out quite as I hoped for—there was this one girl who was offered three bowls!—eventually everyone had his or her bowl. Then again we did a round of striking bowls. It was amazing to see that every child appeared to be very happy with the sound and at the end of the experiment, they were almost unstoppable. The whole energy was very different, pleasant, and relaxed.

This kind of sessions can be basic for a whole, special process, individually or in groups. You might come up with combinations, such as after creating the sounds, having the children expressing themselves on paper with drawings, or free movement along with the sounds of the singing bowls. If you do not have any bowls at your disposal, a CD with sounds of singing bowls may be used as well with these experiments. For instance, you could treat a child that is often very restless with a sound experience while lying in between large speakers. At first, try it for only for a few minutes, and after the child is habited to the sound, give a treatment of up to fifteen minutes. Always stay in touch, because the child needs to keep a feeling of safety all the time.

Children have boundless imaginations. Always try to stimulate these fantasies, in all experiments you do with the singing bowls.[24]

It goes without saying that you can think of a whole range of new possibilities for using singing bowls with children in special situations. What would you think of surrounding premature babies with the sounds of singing bowls, or for that matter, even pregnant women?

Part 5

TINGSHAWS, DORJE, AND BELL

• • • • • • •

"Farewell," said the fox. "This is my secret, it is very simple: You can only see well with your heart. The essence of things is invisible to the eyes."

A. de Saint-Exupéry, *The Little Prince*

29 Tingshaws

If you go to a concert or massage therapist who uses singing bowls, you will usually come across the penetrating singing sound of tingshaws.

Like singing bowls, these small cymbals, which are usually attached to either end of a cord or leather thong, are ritual artifacts. They are used by Buddhist monks but are also used in the shamanic tradition. It is no longer clear who first used them but it is known that in general they are made of seven metals, just like singing bowls. In tingshaws, however, the iron is replaced by meteorite, the "celestial" metal that is taken from fragments of meteors and gives the instruments their pearly shine. Unfortunately, meteorite is a raw material that is only available in very limited quantities because of its very nature, and therefore not all tingshaws contain this metal. The final alloy is cast and turned to obtain a pure form and sound.

Tingshaws are available in different sizes, each with their own sound. Most are smooth, but there are also decorated tingshaws, such as those with patterns of dragons and with the eight symbols of happiness, the Ashtamangalas (see illustration on this page).

Meditational Use

The sound of tingshaws is like a summons. It brings us to the here and now. In meditation, tingshaws are used to indicate the beginning and the end. At the beginning, you let go of everything except the clean moment of here and now; at the end, you should awaken physically and spiritually in the here and now of material reality.

In Tibetan Buddhist meditation rituals, tingshaws are used in different ways. One way is as a summons: the Buddha in one of his aspects, a deity, or a spirit is summoned by the sound, while the sound is also an offering to the summoned being.

Tingshaws are tapped together at right angles for a loud penetrating effect. Dangling horizontally, with the sides exactly touching each other, they produce a softer, light singing sound. They can also be tapped individually with a hard wooden or metal rod. When you do this you can clearly hear the subtle difference in pitch that tingshaws often have and that produces the shimmering effect of the sound.

Another use is in meditation exercises. Just as a master is meant to call back any pupil who has wandered off the path of a Zen meditation exercise, back to the here and now, by tapping him on the shoulders with a bamboo stick, the master in Tibetan monasteries calls a pupil who has wandered away back with the sound of tingshaws, which are alternately sounded on the left and on the right, at right angles to each other, and then held with one of them upright in front of each pupil's eyes. Not only the pupil who has wandered but everyone else who is present is also immediately brought back to the center of their meditation in this way.

Ritual Use

One of the very special uses of the evocative properties of ting-shaws takes place in the ritual known as "The Ceremony of the Hungry Spirits." Very little is known about this ritual. Hans de Back describes it as follows:

> During his life, an unusual spiritual master had a tingshaw that is kept in a special little box after his death. This is a single disc on a plaited cord of silver, coral, and turquoise, with a piece of bone (traditionally belonging to the deceased owner), at the end that serves to tap the tingshaw.
>
> The ceremony is as follows: a particular number of monks (4, 7, or 12) go to the banks of the lake. They sing harmonics and sound the tingshaw twice or three times. In this way they summon the spirit of the owner. It is not permitted to have direct visual contact with the spirit. That is why the monks wear special hoods over their faces so that they can only see the surface of the water and the reflections in it.
> The spirit is probably summoned for a special spiritual lesson that enables the monks to consider their problems from a different perspective.
>
> When the spirit wishes to break the contact, the monks sing subharmonics, which are so shimmering that they cause a wave to rise up on the water. The wave helps the spirit to separate itself from the earthly level to which it has been summoned.

Therapeutic Use

Although we did not describe any specific therapeutic uses for the singing bowls, an exception should be used in the case of the tingshaws for one special application of this pure and purifying sound. Nowadays we know quite a lot about auras, and what can be done for auras. When our body of flesh and blood, which we usually simply call "the body," is disturbed, we know what we can do ourselves or who we have to go to for help. But a person does not consist only of his physical body and aura. There are several bodies. One of these is the so-called ethereal body. This

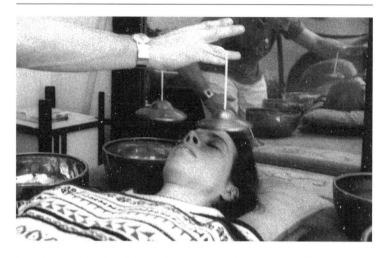

is right next to the skin and many people can actually see it as a white, rather woolly outline slightly bigger than the physical body.

This ethereal body functions as a universal information filter. In other words, all outside information of any sort is received by this body and passed on to the right place. In this way everything that comes to us from outside can be properly assimilated so that we can react to it appropriately. Someone with a whole ethereal body is always able to cope with anything that happens to him or her and to respond in a suitable way. This person will also have a great resistance to panic. When there are weaknesses or holes in the ethereal body, his or her reactions to external stimuli can change considerably. They are slower, or inappropriate, and the person is more likely to panic.

Holes in the ethereal body are particularly caused by drugs (including so-called "soft drugs") and certain allopathic medicines such as antibiotics. The ethereal body does have the capacity to heal but when the holes are large, this capacity is also weakened and it will be a very long time before it is completely healed. Sound, particularly the sound of tingshaws, can be a great help in this. This sort of sound treatment can soon help to form a new network of connecting threads so that the holes are repaired more easily and quickly.

People who have been treated with different tingshaws in a special order of sounds, feel better straight away and more comfortable and wholly in their body.

Another useful application of tingshaws is based on the purifying effect of the sounds. By sounding the tingshaws in the four corners of a room, the energy present in the room is dissolved in the vibration of sound, and the room is once more open and neutral.

30 Dorje and Bell

The bell is an instrument that summons the spirits and deities in the same way as tingshaws. In Shamanism, bells are used to summon spirits: their sound represents the element of air, the realm of the spirits. In Buddhist *pujas* (prayer services), the bell is sounded at the moment that the form of the Buddha for which the ritual is held, is present in the room. The sound of the bell is seen as an offering to the Buddha.

Bells are made of bronze, often containing silver; the sound is partly determined by the silver content of the bell. The choice of the sound is a very personal matter. As a lama told me: "You must go by the feeling of your own heart."

However, anyone who sees the bell only as an instrument of sound is missing its greatest significance in the Tibetan Buddhist tradition, usually in a symbolic unity with the dorje.

To understand this we must first know a little more about Buddhism.

The center of the Buddhist philosophy concerns the Four Noble Truths: 1) we suffer because we are attached to earthly existence; 2) the causes of suffering are desire, hatred, and ignorance; 3) suffering can be relieved; 4) this can be achieved by destroying its cause. Every person can achieve enlightenment by following the right path.

In fact, every Buddhist school is part of one of the three main movements or "vehicles": Hinayana, Mahayana, and Vajrayana or Tantrayana. In Mahayana and Tantrayana, it is assumed that total salvation can only be achieved when every living being has been enlightened. Anyone who seeks enlightenment does so for the benefit for all living creatures. Lamas are the human enlightened guides on this path. Representations of buddhas (principles of enlightenment), transcendental bodhisattvas (physical aspects of help and compassion), and gods (the personification of all aspects of human nature) serve as a support. They are accompanied by a multiplicity of symbolic objects.

The combination of method and wisdom is a basic principle of Tantrism. The method is seen particularly as compassion, wisdom as the consciousness that can conceive of the void. This term "the void" means that nothing stands alone. Everything we perceive exists only because there is something that causes it. The bell (Sanskrit: *ghanta*; Tibetan: *dril bhu*) and the diamond scepter or thunderbolt (Sanskrit: *vajra*; Tibetan: *dorje*) are the symbols of wisdom and method. The dorje is a symbol of the indestructible, the male principle, the means of salvation. The bell is a symbol of the void, the female principle, wisdom. When these two come together, an inner mystical unity is achieved.

In puja (group prayer, offertory service) and sadhana (individual method of self-realization), the bell and dorje are used in the ritual gestures, the *mudras*. When the person performing the ritual wishes to express inner mystical unity, he crosses his hands at the level of his heart in the *mahamudra,* which expresses a state of being that embodies the most complete enlightenment. (*Maha* = large, *mu* = void of wisdom, *dra* = everything. *Mahamudra* is usually translated simply as "large symbol.") In Tibetan, it is usually called *tab sherab. Tab* is the meditation of insight into the void, expressed by the bell; *sherab* is the meditation of the skilled method, expressed by the dorje. In the Tantric tradition, the dorje and the bell are actually specifically tools of the lama, because only a lama with a high level of self-realization permanently resides in tab sherab, and only a lama can transmit this mystical state to other living creatures. It is only when a pupil has received sufficient initiations from the lama on the path of enlightenment, that he may use his own bell and dorje, according to the Tantric tradition.

It is assumed that merely holding the sacred objects does not have any effect at all. The effect is achieved only when the heart is able to assimilate the symbolic significance and make room for it.

Anyone who is attracted by the pure sound of the bell, and has bought one to use it as an object for meditation, can at least try to assimilate this symbolic significance as much as possible. The void is symbolized by the sound. In fact, this sound is not an independent entity; it is only created when there is a bell, a clapper, and someone who brings the two together. The sound follows from this contact. Therefore the sound is created from the void and then disappears into the void.

This is an exercise you could do with the bell: empty your mind, so that everything that is in it falls away. When your mind is as empty as possible, sound the bell. Listen how the sound is made, how it resonates, and how it finally ends.

In Shamanism, the bell is sometimes sounded by rubbing a stick round the edge; this produces a high singing tone.

The bell and dorje are only external symbols of an inner state of being, but their appearance itself is also symbolic; every part has a meaning.

These meanings are briefly summarized on the following pages. For a more detailed description of all the aspects concerned, refer to *The Book of Buddhas*, which includes a complete survey of the five "Buddha families."

Dorje
In a so-called "peaceful" dorje, the ends of the spokes come together; in an "wrathful" dorje, the spokes are separate. Ritual objects such as the bell, dagger, and hatchet have a handle with one knob of a dorje; individual separate dorjes have two knobs; there are also double dorjes *vishavajra*) with four knobs, but these are rare and almost only found in illustrations. The top half of the dorje represents the male side; the bottom half is the female side.

From top to bottom, we see the following aspects:

First, there are the five spokes, the symbol of the five Jinas (transcendental Buddhas), which represent the five forms of mystical wisdom. The four spokes on the outside each emerge from the open maw of a sea monster; this symbolizes the liberation from the cycle of reincarnation.

Underneath there is a hemisphere with eight lotus leaves, representing the eight Bodhisattvas.

The center of the dorje is a globe, the symbol of synthesis, the point in which everything is enclosed.

The bottom half of the dorje is the mirror image of the top half. Here, the eight lotus leaves represent the eight dakinis (also called goddesses) of the Bodhisattvas, and the five spokes symbolize the five Buddhadakinis, or "mothers."

The Bell

The handle of the bell is the knob of the dorje, resting on a moon disc. Underneath there is a face.

According to one view, this is the face of the goddess or female Bodhisattva, Prajnaparamita, the incarnation of complete transcendental wisdom; according to another view, it is the face of Viarocana, the incarnation of universal truth, dharma.

Looking at the outside of the bell from above, you see a mandala (illustrated in the circle on page 117).

From the center down to the edge, this contains the following components: a circle of eight lotus leaves, which forms the mandala of the voice of the gods, with the mantras of the five

Jinas written in the leaves. There is a broad decorative strip all around this, which often contains dorjes.

The outer (bottom) edge is filled with exactly 51 dorjes, which represent the 51 small unknowns that can be resolved by the effect of the bell.

The sound mantra of the bell is the AOUM sound, which symbolizes perfection and is seen as the sound of the body, voice, and spirit of Buddha, as well as being a symbol of the voice of all the gods together.

31 Iconographics

In the rich iconography of Mahayana and Tantrayana, the dorje and bell are common images. The dorje is often seen without the bell, and with other attributes, but the bell is rarely found without the dorje. For example, the Buddha Amitabha, in tantric union with his female partner (prajna) uses a bell and a begging bowl, in which an ashoka tree is germinating as a symbol of the carefree beatitude of the interim paradise Sukhavati, of which Amitabha is the lord.

Buddha Amoghasiddhi uses the bell and the sword, the symbolic destroyer of ignorance in illustrations in which he is shown in tantric union with his prajna, Tara.

Some illustrations of Vairocana show the combination of the bell and dharmachakra (the wheel of truth).

Vairocana, who is sometimes seen as the original Buddha, is called Vajradhara when he is depicted in the classical mahamudra with the bell and dorje.

Vajrasattva is shown in a different position with the bell and dorje.

In Nepal, this buddha is seen as the original Buddha, who was there before all the others, the "Lord who was created from himself." In Tibet he is called "Dorje Sempa," and he is seen as the essence of the body of all Buddhas. With him, the dorje and bell are symbols of perfect compassion and perfect wisdom, and his prayer is that of perfect joy. He is illustrated on page 128.

32 The Lama at Work

It is an exceptional experience to see the lama at work with the dorje and bell. It is described in words of wonder and respect in many books about Tibet and Tibetan Buddhism. I shared in this experience when I visited Lama Gawang in Lelystad, the Netherlands. His magnificent bell and dorje, decorated with turquoise, were lying in front of him on a garden table in the sun. Lama Gawang explained to me what he was doing.

"The bell is the female side; the dorje is the male side. But the female heart points to the right, and the male heart points to the left, therefore we place the dorje to the left, and the bell to the right, in front of us."

When the lama performs this ritual for himself, the face on the bell is pointing toward him, but if it is meant for others, he turns this face away, toward them.

First, the dorje is picked up with the right hand, the male hand, and then the bell is picked up with the left hand, the female hand. The lama's hands described beautifully stylized arcs, in which the dorje and the bell constantly changed position in an easy, flowing movement.

The lama explained, "The movements of the hands symbolize the activities of the gods while they are dancing." My attention was completely taken up with the dance, but the movements were over before I had a chance to see them properly.

The lama crossed his hands over his chest with a light, serene smile. He said, "The dorje is held slightly higher than the bell. This is *tab sherab*. *Tab* makes the ego smaller; *sherab* purifies it. When the ego has gone, all suffering is dissolved. It is the work of the lamas to perform this; it is the work of the pupil to meditate and take the power from the ego.

The lama is the guide. Tilopa, the founder of our order of the Kagyupas, said to his pupil, 'I have shown you the way how to go to the Buddha. But you will have to go yourself.' "

CONCLUSION

• • • • • • •

Only the sound—
but then it was an evening
of summer rain

Issa
(Japanese Haiku poet)

The water in the bowl gleams

I strike the rim of the bowl softly at first and then slightly harder. At first slowly, but then in faster cadences...

The water in the bowl is ruffled in a fine herring-bone pattern; the same endlessly repeated pattern that is engraved on the side of the bowl.

Suddenly the miracle happens again. Drops of water shoot up in four places, higher and higher, until the round, silver drops spray out several inches above the rim of the bowl and then fall back into the bowl with a clear, splashing sound accompanying the familiar singing of the bowl, with their sparkling sound.

I do not know where this bowl came from, when it was made, by whom, or why. After much study and research I still do not know. I do not know whether the maker meant to create these delightful effects when he shaped the bowl, with the hammer blows that are still visible, and when he engraved the decorations and applied the matte black layer of varnish that is now half worn away.

Perhaps he would laugh in bewilderment if he saw what I was doing. Perhaps he would be happy that his work was still being used. Perhaps he would think I was stupid because it is so obvious that I do not understand. But why should I care?

What is important, is the sound.

NOTES

The italics used in Alexandra David Neel's story are just as the author used them. In the following notes I have quoted only the parts that are necessary for a proper understanding of the text.

1. A follower of the Bön religion.
2. The *chang* (written as *gchang)* is a musical instrument that is especially used by *bönpos*. It is roughly the same shape as a cymbal, with the edges bent inward and it has a clapper. It is played with the clapper pointing upwards like an upturned bell.
3. Written as *gzungs:* something that grips, holds onto. A magic formula. The Sanskrit equivalent is *dharani mantra.*
4. Written as *phyirolpa:* outsiders, meaning people who are not Buddhists, followers of another faith. It refers here specifically to the Brahmin Hindus.
5. Belonging to the Dzogchen sect (written as *rdzogstchen):* "great fulfillment." The most recently established Tibetan sect.
6. Written as *grubthob:* someone who possesses supernatural powers. The Tibetan equivalent of the Sanskrit *Siddha* or *Siddhi purucha.*
7. Refers to the Tibetan creation myths, in which the wind *(rlung,* pronounced lung*)* is not the wind as we know it, but the movement of the first forms, the *gyatams* (written as *rgya Pram* or *rgua gram).* The lamas depict these *gyatams* as *dorjis* intertwined in the shape of the cross, whilst the *bönpos* represent them as swastikas—the symbol of movement. The man with whom I spoke was a white *bön.*
8. *Gyu,* written as *rgyu:* matter, substance.
9. This means that the sound that can destroy the basic principle, the origin of the created world, is the fundamental sound, the subtle sound from which all destructive sounds are derived.

10. David Lindner, *Das Geheimnis der Klangschalen*, ISBN 3-933825-21-0.

11. Two Germans: Peter Hess and Frank Plate. Hess, who also wrote a standard work about singing bowls, has his own import brand (ACAMA) and trains people to become sound therapists. Plate has specialized in planet singing bowls (read chapter 26) and sound massage.

12. See www.steinklang.de/klangschalen/klangschalen.htm for examples of a wide range of singing bowls.

13. The word "resonate" comes from the Latin *re-sonare*, "sounding along with the original source."

14. Unfortunately there are many low quality CDs on the market: bad recordings, bad sound quality, bad tuning, and bad attitude. So before you buy these recordings as a layman it is recommended you first check and feel and compare what is offered, but also ask for advice from experts in the field.

15. You can find various exercises in the book *Healing Sounds* by Jonathan Goldman (see Reading List).

16. This happens just the same with music you listen to with an MP3 player or other modern storage equipment; the very low and the very high frequencies are filtered out to save more storage room.

17. Read further about the practice of singing along with the bowls in chapter 18. You can also find more information in the books by Jonathan Goldman, Frank Perry, and Dick de Ruiter (see Reading List).

18. Read more about this in chapter 18 and in *Harmonic Overtones in Voice and Music* by Dick de Ruiter.

19. An extended exploration about these crystal singing bowls—including a CD—is *Crystal & Sound* by de Ruiter.

20. You can hear these tones of the planets on singing bowls on the CDs from Rainer Tillmann, *The Sounds of the Planets*, and with large gongs on the sound massage CDs by David Lindner.

21. Read more about this in *Sounds Like OM*, by Dick de Ruiter.

22. Anneke Huyser and Don Campbell have included many delightful meditations and sound exercises in their books (see Reading List).

23. Read more about this in *Yoga & Sound* by Dick de Ruiter.
24. The use of singing bowls to help children with ADD and ADHD is a new method. Read more about this in *Healing Sounds for ADHD* by Dick de Ruiter.

SOURCES AND BIBLIOGRAPHY

Sources: Hans de Back, Danny Becher, Lisa Borstlap, Erik Bruijn, Binkey Kok, Dries Langeveld, Joska Soos.
With thanks to Ronald Chavers for the many years of teaching on Shamanism.

AC Bhaktivedanta Swami Prabhupada. *Bhagavad-gita As It Is.* Los Angeles: Bhaktivedanta Book Trust, 1972

Berendt, Joachim-Ernst. *Brahma: The World Is Sound; Music and the Landscape of Consciousness.* Rochester, VT: Destiny Books, 1987

Boenders, Frans. *Tibetaans Dagboek.* Brussels: BRT, 1987

Bruijn, Erik. *Tantra, Yoga en Meditatie: De Tibetaanse weg naar verlichting.* Deventer: Ankh-Hermes, 1980

David-Néel, Alexandra. *Au pays des brigades-gentilshommes.* Paris: Plon, 1933

Dixon, Terence, and Tony Buzan. *The Evolving Brain.* New York: Holt, Rinehart & Winston, 1977

Hoff, Benjamin. *The Tao of Pooh.* New York: Dutton, 1982

Khan, Hazrat Inayat. *Music.* Surrey: Farnham, Sufi, 1962

Lama Lödö. *Bardo Teachings: the Way of Death and Rebirth.* Ithaca, NY: Snow Lion Publications, 1982

Langeveld, Dries. 'Het raadsel van de zingende schalen,' in: BRES 10 (Oct.-Nov. 1986)

Langeveld, Dries. 'De Kristallen Bol,' in: BRES 157 (Dec.-Jan. 1992/1993)

Lao Tzu. *The Tao Te Ching.* New York: Paragon House, 1989

ONKRUID 61 (March-April 1988): Jubileumthema 'Muziek, feest en verklankte spiritualiteit' (pages 63-101)

PRANA 53 (Fall 1988): Themanummer 'Muziek en Muziektherapie'

Saint-Exupéry, A. de. *The Little Prince.* New York: Reynal and Hitchcock, 1943

Soos, Joska. *Ik genees niet, ik herstel de harmonie* (samenge-
    steld en bewerkt door Robert Hartzema). Amsterdam: Kar-
    nak, 1985
Tarthang Tulku. *Hidden Mind of Freedom.* Berkeley: Dharma
    Publishing, 1981
Temple, Robert K.G. *China: Land of Discovery.* Wellingbor-
    ough: Stephens, 1986
Tooren, J. van. *Haiku Een jonge maan.* Amsterdam: Meulen-
    hoff, 1973

The character that marks the last pages of the different parts of
this book is the symbol of the universal sound mantra OM.

FURTHER READING

Andrews, Ted. *Sacred Sounds: Magic & Healing Through Words & Music.* Woodbury, MN: Llewellyn Publications, 2002.

Beer, Robert. *Tibetan Ting-Sha: Sacred Sound for Spiritual Growth.* London: Connections Press, 2004.

Bernard, Patrick. *Music as Yoga: Discover the Healing Power of Sound.* San Rafael: Mandala Publications, 2004.

Campbell, Don. *The Mozart Effect.* New York: HarperCollins Publishers, 2001.

Carr, Alistair. *The Singing Bowl: Journeys through Inner Asia.* London: Horse Travel Books, 2006.

Gayner, Mitchell L. *The Healing Power of Sound.* Boston: Shambala Books, 2002.

Goldman, Jonathan. *Healing Sounds: The Power of Harmonics.* Rochester, VT: Healing Arts Press, 2002.

Huyser, Anneke. *Singing Bowls, Exercises for Personal Harmony.* Haarlem (NL): Binkey Kok, 2004.

Leeds, Joshua. *The Power of Sound.* Rochester, VT: Healing Arts Press, 2001.

Lyddon, Andrew. *Working with Singing Bowls: A Sacred Journey.* London: Polair Publishing, 2007.